101^{+} Tips On Writing Fiction

101^{+} Tips On Writing Fiction

Get organized,
Get started and finish that first novel!

Inside these pages you'll find tips and
fill-in-the-blank worksheets to help you
plan and create the Great American Novel,

plus *marketing tips on selling your finished novel to*
agents, editors and readers.

PRUDY TAYLOR BOARD

and

RUTH HARTMAN BERGE

Cover art and logo by Scott Shamblin

ISBN: 1547174633
ISBN-13: 978-1547174638

DEDICATIONS

To Jennifer and Byron. The only time my talents as a writer fail me are when I try to describe how grateful I am and how loved my children are.

Prudy Taylor Board

For Margaret Hartman who once held my hand as I learned to form letters and has patiently read every story I've written ever since.
Thanks, Mom!

Ruth Hartman Berge.

FOREWORD

For 40$^+$ years, I've earned by livelihood as a writer. The world has changed and so has the means of delivering text to readers, but much has remained the same. So much so, in fact, that I feel this previously published foreword is worth sharing for 21st century writers.

You've heard it. You've been to a cocktail party…or a church social…or a scouting outing when someone says nonchalantly, "I could write a novel. And I'm going to. Just as soon as I have time." No one ever says, "I've always wanted to be a brain surgeon and I'm going to begin operating. Just as soon as I have a little time."

Of course, there's a big difference. (I know—writers don't bury their mistakes—although sometimes we'd like to!) There's also a similarity. In each instance, you must know what you're doing. And, in each profession, you will find elements of both craft and art. Luck plays a major role in a writer's career as well.

This book will not presume to teach you the ART of writing a novel—only Divine Intelligence can create the tree and the truly gifted author.

RED ALERT: If you're expecting any form of academic treatise, stop! Put this book down. Return it to the shelf. If you're looking for practical information, carry on. You see, craft can be learned. And in these pages, hopefully, you'll find a modicum of inspiration, lots of encouragement and an abundance of useful information. It's a very personal book because it contains all the things I've learned the hard way—by rejections, by trial and error, by making mistakes. It's a book I wish I'd had when I started out. And this book contains much of the information included 101 Tips. Thanks to Ruth's fine work we've added information on marketing and promotion, updated the recommended reading list as well as writer's organizations we think might be helpful.

BONUS TIP: No extra charge! A sense of humor is absolutely essential if you're going to survive in the writer's world. And if you don't have one, begin cultivating it now.

Why? Because there are going to be many times when you won't know whether to laugh or cry. However, in the long run, tears and anger and feelings of personal rejection are not only nonproductive, but a waste of our most precious commodity—time.

So learn to laugh at the rejections, at the slights…this is a tough business. You'll find an abundance of people who'll tell you your talent is not "significant" or that you'll never make it as a writer. Paste a smile on your face. Thank them nicely—success is the best response. Then get back to your work…which is writing and constantly learning to write more effectively and efficiently.

And keep writing.

Always.

That's what successful professional writers do, you know.

They write.

Day in, day out, they write.

Headaches, backaches, heartaches, stomach aches, they write.

By all means, keep us posted. If you have any questions or comments, email us at info@101pluswritingtips.com. When you sell that splendid first novel, drop us a note so we can cheer with you. We might even hoist a glass of champagne in your honor!

Prudy Taylor Board
Delray Beach Florida
April, 2017

I was thrilled to be invited to join with Prudy Taylor Board in the updating of her book of tips on writing and selling your first novel. I first met Prudy in 2011 when I had finally decided it was time to do the one thing I had wanted to do my entire life—write. Like most people, I never seemed to find enough time to get around to it until one day it hit me that the years had slipped by and it was a now or never type of thing. When I met Prudy, I was a blogger and a columnist with dreams of writing that first book. I bought the first edition of _101 Tips for Writing and Selling Your First Novel._ Using those tips, I self-published one book, had a second one published by The History Press (Arcadia) and completed my first murder mystery.

I'm sharing this with you because you can do what I did. It takes work, but you can do it. The tips in this book are a solid roadmap to completing that novel you've always dreamed of writing.

Prudy asked me to tag along with some marketing tips because writing and selling your book to an agent or publisher is only part of the process. You need to interest readers in buying your book without driving them insane with constant pleas. It's a delicate art, but one that can be a lot of fun.

If you're still reading, then turn the page and let the adventure begin! The day you hold a book in your hand that displays your name as author will be one of the happiest days of your life. And yes, let us know so we can join you in the happy hamster dance!

Ruth Hartman Berge
Jupiter, Florida
April, 2017

ACKNOWLEDGMENTS

We would like to thank the authors who tirelessly worked to write the books we have both devoured over our lifetimes and our agents and editors who bought and rejected our books—they taught us so much.

We would also like to thank Joanne Sinchuk, bookseller extraordinaire, of Murder on the Beach Mystery Bookstore in Delray Beach, Florida—not only for her support of us—but of all authors who darken the bookstore's door.

TABLE OF CONTENTS

CHAPTER 7: IT'S EASIER SEEN IN A SCENE   57

CHAPTER 8: GETTING AHEAD IN TIME AND PLACE A/K/A   61
TRANSITION AND EXPOSITION

CHAPTER 9: FINAL (W)RITES AND OTHER ET CETERA   65

CHAPTER 10: ONE LAST REMINDER ABOUT EDITS…   69

CHAPTER 11: TO MARKET TO MARKET

CHAPTER 12: SURVIVAL TECHNIQUES

CHAPTER 13: PRE-PUBLICATION MARKETING

CHAPTER 1: GETTING READY TO WRITE

We may never know whether the chicken or the egg came first, but we do know that the idea always comes before the novel. We also know that splendid ideas for novels may arrive at any time, in any place. Further, we know that when we're going through a barren stage, we must know how to cultivate ideas.

Now how about you? Do you know how to manipulate both your mind and your muse to come up with ideas?

The process is not difficult, but it involves a degree of personal discomfort because it requires change. To encourage ideas, you must begin by training yourself to think like a writer. Don't fall into a routine. If you must travel to the same destination every day, take different routes. Make new friends. Constantly expose yourself to new groups of people, to new places, to new ideas. Live as a writer. Discipline yourself to look at all human situations as possible plots and everyone you meet as a potential character.

If you do, you'll be amazed by the different ways ideas can descend, debark, implode, explode in your life. You may see a scene—an argument between a beautiful couple in a restaurant, a child of divorced parents waiting to be picked up by the other parent, a bad accident—that triggers the idea for a novel. You may meet a person who is so dynamic, so interesting, so offbeat and eccentric or charming and naïve or manipulative, that you immediately envision him or her as the protagonist of your book.

Smell, taste, touch and remember

Sometimes a sensory experience can trigger an idea for a novel. Perhaps you smell a fragrance or an odor that's unusual. Don't scoff. *Perfume*, a brilliant best seller by Patrick Suskind, focused on the sense of smell. Perhaps you touch a piece of fabric that evokes memories or sensations. Or maybe you see a piece of jewelry or antique furniture that reminds you of something your grandmother had. In other words, a sensory experience that gives you an idea. An article about a new medical treatment for an exotic disease or a breakthrough in genetics triggers an idea for a book. Perhaps you work better by beginning with a theme, a statement: Love is stronger than evil. If so, take a premise important to you and work from that.

Ideas are everywhere: Just open your mind, your eyes, your ears, and your heart. Develop the habit of listening to conversations. And don't worry—eavesdropping isn't a crime. (If it is a crime, it's a misdemeanor. So don't worry about it, just be subtle.) Watch television, read several newspapers, read magazines, force yourself to stay alert to what's on the minds and the hearts of people today because that's what tells you what editors are looking for, what they want to buy.

Use your passport.

Always ask yourself that wonderful question, "What if?" Those two words are passports to wonderful worlds for writers. Carry a notebook or some 3 x 5 cards and jot down your ideas the moment they strike—don't lose them! If you drive a lot, keep a digital recorder on your front seat and dictate your ideas.

When you have a block of time, on a weekend for example, type out your notes. Expand each into a couple of paragraphs. Then one evening when you have a little time, sift through them. Don't just tuck them away, refer to them often, read and reread them during this period. The visual images, the fragment of sparkling dialogue, the unique phrases, the unusual slogans, the amusing, revealing gestures—whatever comprises the corpus of your notes will meld into a plot idea you can use during this gestation period. Does one idea grab at you, won't let you go? Look at it, study it, think about it. Give the idea a little time to germinate and cool down—a day or two.

Look at your notes again.

You now must test your idea to see if it has enough gravitas, enough complexity, relevance to you and your readers as well as intrigue. In short, is it worth developing into a full-length novel? Ask yourself if the story idea will still be current and interesting two to five years from now. You must think in terms of that length of time because once you've written and sold the book, it can take up to two years to reach the bookstores and newsstands. This means your idea must be something you believe in and it cannot be based on a fad. Ask yourself, too, if you will enjoy working on this idea for a long period of time. If the idea is not going to hold your interest, don't feel you must develop and write it.

Think about the characters who will live in your pages and tell your story. Are they interesting? Are these people you enjoy? Do you want to spend anywhere from six months to two or three years with them? Are they exciting and interesting? If not, can you work with them so that they come to life and breathe? Remember that being lifelike isn't enough. Your characters must be people your readers will cheer for, tremble when they're in jeopardy, and boo and hiss when they do dirty deeds.

Now consider where your book will take place. Is it a setting with a regional flavor that strangers will want to learn more about or is it an exotic setting? Must you create a fictional town? If so, where will it be? Is it a city or a village? Give it a name.

And the time frame. How much time will your book span? How long is it going to take you to tell this story, not to write it, but to tell it within the covers of the book. On what date does your story begin and end?

When you reach the point where you can answer these questions, you're ready to write a detailed synopsis in which you work through the basic storyline. This can range from 5 to 35 double-spaced pages.

Remember: this is a synopsis, not a detailed working outline. We'll get to that shortly. For the moment, you're creating a synopsis in which you work out the major plotline, settle on your most important scenes and decide who your major characters will be.

Bottom line: A synopsis is the narrative of your book. It contains very little if any dialogue. (If you've never written a synopsis, don't worry. See page 76 for the format.)

By now, you should be committed to your project. Your next step will be to create files for your prepubescent creation. Start files for characters, settings, markets, the working outline, and research materials on any topic you think you'll need. Give your book a working title. Bear in mind, this probably won't be your final title, it's just temporary. Chances are 50-50 that the publisher or the publisher's marketing department will change the title.

Don't rush to your computer. You're still not ready!

Tip #1. Writer's block is not created because the fickle muse leaves you when you need her most.

Writer's block usually arises either because you are writing too soon—that is, you haven't done the necessary research to figure out where you're going with the story or because you're writing a book you think you *should* write, not one you want to write.

To work through writer's block, begin by working out the bugs in your plot by making a detailed chapter-by-chapter, scene-by-scene outline. This is the outline from which you will work so it's worth taking the time to get it right.

Some writers don't like to work from outlines because they maintain it destroys spontaneity. They insist they like to discover what's going to happen simultaneously with their characters. You may get to that point, but in the beginning you are wise to create a complete outline for several reasons.

First: Outlining enables you to make choices. Instead of writing to the end without knowing what's going to happen, instead of desperately ending it the best way you can think of at the moment, if you plan ahead, you can look at all your options and decide which will be most satisfying for your reader and truest to your characters. You can also work out what will be most truthful and unified from the standpoint of the plot and the theme of your book.

Second: An outline is indispensable if you have to leave a book-in-progress for a few days, weeks or months and come back to it. For example, if your work is interrupted by a death in the family, unexpected company, an illness or vacation, you can get back into your book much quicker if you have a detailed outline.

Third: An outline gives you a wonderful sense of security: You know you can finish the book. And you know how you're going to do it. Furthermore, you won't end up with file cabinets full of unfinished novels. (How do you find out if you should work with an outline? There's a simple test: Open your desk drawer. If it's filled with unfinished 50-page manuscripts, you need to outline.)

Fourth and finally: Writing from an outline and pre-planning your novel frees you to focus on the quality of your writing.

You must now become good at handling your writing time. From now on, you don't want to write anything that's not going to sell, and you don't want to write anything that you're going to have to labor over time and time again to get right. Get it right at least the third time through—that's another perk from prior planning. The pre-planning you're doing at this point will not only make the initial writing easier and more effective, it can substantially cut your revision time. And you'll find you'll start selling more regularly when you start planning your writing.

Writing is work. Don't waste your time and energy on a 50-page novel that goes nowhere. Outline!

Keep in mind that your outline is not etched in marble. If you get a better idea as you go along, that's terrific. Just make sure your new idea is consistent with the plot and the tone of your book as well as the characters you've developed.

Now, here's how to outline. First, take your synopsis and break it into scenes and chapters. (Don't worry too much about the specifics of outlining, you'll find an example on page 9.)

Let's think a moment about scenes and chapters. The scenes in your book are those sections where you have action, where you show your characters talking, doing, fighting, loving. A scene has a beginning, a middle and an end—a structure. You can begin the scene with the dramatic moment in the beginning, the middle or the end.

Say your scene involves John and Frank arguing. They become so enraged they strike one another. You can open the scene at a quiet moment when John walks into the men's store where Frank works. Their conversation deteriorates into verbal insults, then escalates into shoving and pushing. The scene ends where the two slug it out. Or you can begin with Frank and John slugging it out, then they start talking and John leaves determined to get revenge on Frank. Or the scene can open with the two men arguing, the middle is the fistfight and the scene ends when John leaves. Here you have merely shifted the moment of maximum emotion; in so doing, you have altered the structure of the scene.

Strive for variety in your scenes both from the standpoint of length and structure.

Remember: You don't want to be predictable.

How do you decide when to start a new chapter? And what is a chapter? The answer: A chapter can be a collection of scenes. Or it can contain only one scene. A chapter is an artificial division of your book. It can be long or short. It's as long as it takes you to write or portray the action in this sequence.

Here are some general rules: Group scenes in a chapter when they are happening continuously, when there is little or no time elapsing between them. Start a new chapter after you have a significant period of time in which nothing important happens. Your hero goes to sleep. If nothing happens during the night, end the chapter when he nods off. Start a new chapter the next day when the action begins again, when something interesting and relevant happens. Start a new scene when you have changed your point-of-view character or cast of characters. In some instances, you start a new scene when the setting changes.

A word of warning: You and your novel are most vulnerable at the end of a chapter. This is when most readers are programmed to put your book down. The end of a chapter is a good stopping point for them, but you mustn't let them do this to you and your splendid book!

Try to plan your book so that your reader must read on. You can do this by leaving various subplots in mid-crises. Or by deliberately leaving the conflict in a scene unresolved. For example, if your heroine is poised on the ledge of an apartment building, be brutal. Leave her there a while. End the chapter. (We call this a hook.) Open your next chapter with a scene involving your hero or one of your secondary characters. A chapter or two later return to your heroine on the ledge. (Suspense keeps readers turning those pages!)

While in the planning stage, you must make some decisions about each scene. Unless you're writing a book from the viewpoint of one character, you'll have to decide (and write down) the name of the viewpoint character for each scene. If you're not sure who your viewpoint character should be, think about the action of the scene and decide through which character's eyes you can most efficiently show it. In the scene with John and Frank, either would work.

Next, decide on the location of the scene. Is it going to take place in the Post Office? The reptile cage at the Columbus Zoo? Is it going to take place in the middle of Fifth Avenue? Is it going to take place in Madonna's living room? Write down the location.

Now decide what time the action takes place. Is it morning, late afternoon? Is it dinnertime? Midnight? And what is the climate like? What is the tone of the scene? Is it physical with a lot of action? Or cerebral and introspective? Note that as well.

Your next mission is to write a one to three sentence summary of the action that takes place in that scene. For instance: The first scene of chapter one is a surprise birthday party that takes place at 8 p.m. in the heroine's home on Hibiscus Drive. Attending are her friends and the people who work for her in the bookstore she inherited from her parents. At the end of the scene, the hero (a police lieutenant) calls to tell her the store's been broken into and to ask her to come down to the shop to see what, if anything, has been stolen.

Finally, write a phrase or two to state the purpose of the scene. In each scene, you must accomplish more than one purpose. In the first scene described above, you introduced the hero, the heroine and her friends. You established that her parents are dead so that right away the reader knows she's alone and she's vulnerable. Third, you gave your reader a feeling of what and where she is from the standpoint of her career, so in that first scene you know that she owns and operates a bookstore she inherited from her parents. Then, to hook your reader, you included the break-in at the store to introduce a sense of threat and suspense in the very first scene.

It's important to write a very brief summary of the purpose of each scene to help you stay focused. Furthermore, if you know precisely what you must accomplish with each scene, it helps you keep the pace brisk and moving forward. This sense of focus also lends energy and drive to your work because you won't write wandering, rambling scenes that go nowhere and accomplish nothing.

At this point, you may find yourself working on a number of these elements at once—character, plot, setting. Don't be concerned—you can't control the creative process. Relax and let it happen. You'll get information in bits and pieces. Have confidence that you'll be able to put everything together in its proper place.

There's an adage you've undoubtedly heard. It reads: Well begun is half done. For writers, well begun is a good third done. And that makes a major difference when you're facing writing a 250 to 500 page book.

(There's still another old adage: If it's inevitable you're going to be a writer, try to relax and enjoy it!)

Tip #2. First steps.

Your first mental step should be to inventory your writing supplies and to make a list of what you need. Your first physical step should be out your front door to the office supply store. There you'll stock up on the supplies you'll need to turn out this magnificent tome. Sounds a bit simplistic, but this serves three purposes.

First: It helps you prepare psychologically for the project.

Second: It helps you work more efficiently.

Third: It removes temptation.

What temptation?

Fair question. You're working along and things aren't going so well and you decide you need pens or an ink cartridge for your printer. That's an excellent excuse to scoot out the front door.

And once you're out, you might as well run some other errands—stop by the dry cleaners, pick up a quart of milk at the grocery store, take the car in for a tune-up. As a result, you lose hours of good working time and you break your writing rhythm.

An important part of getting a novel written is learning to abort or short circuit nonproductive behavior.

While you're at the office supply store, be sure to pick up a package of small, spiral-ring notebooks and pens. You're going to leave these around your house—on the nightstand by your bed, in the bathroom, on the dining room table, by the telephone, by the chair where you watch television. You'll keep one in your purse or pocket as well. You'll find these invaluable because once you've decided on your book project, your mind shifts into overdrive and you get all sorts of ideas. You'll also need to make a lot of notes about topics to research. Don't lose these gems. This is an especially exciting, productive, creative time and you want to take advantage of every second. Also, while you're at the office supply store, be sure to pick up a package of storage boxes unless you have an empty drawer in a file cabinet.

Storage boxes?

Yes. Or go to your favorite supermarket and pick up several cardboard cartons roughly 8 ½ x 11 or 8 ½ x 14—in other words, big enough to hold the size file folder you prefer to use.

Tip #3. Next, take a storage box...

...and label it with a felt tipped pen in big letters with the working title of your book. Put the box where you will have easy access to it.

Now you've got a place for your research materials. These will include newspaper clippings and magazine articles, maps, pamphlets, interview notes, photographs, materials you've downloaded from the Internet and the file folders with outlines, character sketches and so forth as well as the workbook you create specifically for this novel.

It's also neater. If you're like most writers, you don't have an entire room you can devote to your writing. When you use storage boxes, you only have to put away the first box with your manuscript-in-progress and the second with your supplies. The next morning when you start to work again, you know where to find your manuscript and supplies and they are easily accessible.

Tip #4. There's a place for it, a time and place for it...but when and where?

It's very important that you find a place to write. The secret here is twofold.
First: Find a place where you do nothing but write.
Second: Go there every day.

You can write at the dining room table, that's fine. But don't work where you sit to eat. Choose another place at the table. You are conditioning yourself so that when you go to your writing space, that's automatically what you do. Think about going to work. When you reach your workplace, you work and you work because you've reached your workplace. Conditioning.

Your writing area should not have a beautiful view and it should be quiet. If you must write in the midst of a busy household, try to find a place partially shielded by white noise. White noise is noise without character—the sound of a fan, an air conditioner. The noise is not distracting in and of itself, but acts to partially block or filter extraneous sound.

And before you really get started on this new novel, take time to observe the times of day or night when you are at your maximum level of creativity. Some people percolate first thing in the morning. Others come alive mentally and physically after dark.

Try to schedule your regular writing time at your time of peak performance. If you can't because the real world interferes (and it does that so often), don't be discouraged. Just write some every day at the same time whenever you can schedule it. It's not a perfect world. (Now you didn't know that, did you?)

Tip #5. Time really IS of the essence.

How long do you think it's going to take you to write this novel? Most writers turn out five to eight pages of copy a day. That varies, of course, depending on the writer. Since this is your first book and you're full of enthusiasm, you might think you can do better than that, but be realistic. If you're not used to writing full time and you're trying to juggle a job and a writing career, aim for one or two pages. If you turn out more, great. In the beginning, however, you'll be more productive if you set a realistic goal because you won't establish such high expectations that you get discouraged when you don't or can't meet them.

Once you've figured out how long it's going to take to write the book, establish the date when you think you'll have the first draft done.

Next, take a sheet of paper and write the name of your novel in big letters and the date you anticipate finishing the first draft. Post it prominently in your office so you can see it every day. We all need goals. And we need to be reminded of them.

If you find the idea of having the entire book written by a certain date intimidating, try this: Work on the outline so you have a rough idea of how many chapters it will contain. Then set yourself a goal of writing a chapter a week.

If you think it will have 30 chapters, take a sheet of paper and write CHAPTER ONE on the left. On the right, put the date of the first Friday of the week when you start the novel. On the next line put CHAPTER TWO and opposite the date of the next Friday. Do this through your thirtieth chapter.

As you finish a chapter, mark it off. If you're still intimidated, try making a 3" x 5" card for each scene in your outline. When you sit down to write, take it one card at a time. When you've finished a scene, mark a big X through it.

Tip #6. Map it out.

You've got three choices—either you'll use a real city, town, etc. or you'll make like a real estate developer and create one or you'll use a real town and add-in fictional stores, churches, schools, homes and streets. Whichever you choose, you've got to move your characters through the streets and alleys and highways and, furthermore, you've got to do it consistently. If your character walks out the front door of his home to go to the public library, turns left at the corner of Oak and Elm Streets, proceeds down Elm to Kroger's Drugstore at the intersection of Vine and Ivy Avenues and spots the granite library building with its statue of Abraham Lincoln on the lawn in the middle of Ivy Avenue, two things should happen.

First: The library should remain fixed—it's always in the middle of Ivy Avenue.

Second: Your character should go to the library the same way. Unless, of course, your character takes a short cut and this should be explained to the reader—and there should be a reason for this deviation.

The easiest way to achieve this consistency is to either draw or obtain a map of the area. In either case, you should make a note on the map indicating the locations of the buildings and sites you will be using in your novel. And when you're doing your final revision, one of the things you will check is your geography.

Why is this important?

Another fair question.

Have you ever read a book where the writer goofed? As a reader it not only irritated you, it destroyed or damaged your sense of involvement in the story. As writers, our goal is to create a fictional world so believable that our readers are trapped there, turning page after page until we choose to end the book and release them.

Consistency is an important element in developing that believability.

Tip #7. Write it in your workbook.

What workbook, you ask? The one you're going to make. It doesn't have to be fancy. You can use a Duotang folder or a three-ring notebook such as kids use in school.

Divide your workbook into sections: Chapter-by-chapter outline, calendar, character bios, settings, topics to research, and miscellaneous notes. In this workbook, you'll have a separate page for each chapter.

In another section, you'll have a separate sheet for each major and secondary character on which you'll write their background biographical information.

In the settings section, you'll include the map of the area with the significant roads and buildings and sites marked.

You'll also include your book's calendar, and we'll discuss this in more detail later.

Also, you'll include a section for miscellaneous notes and items such as quotes and poems you might want to use in the front or at chapter headings.

In addition to the notes you make as you begin the novel, this is a working notebook which grows as your novel grows. For example, every time you introduce a character for the first time, make a note in that chapter. And include a brief description. Same with the settings. Then, as you go along, if you need to check to be sure your description is consistent, you'll find it easier to find that first reference.

Also, as you write each chapter, there may be points you want to include or changes you want to make in the revision. You can make these notes right in your workbook and you won't misplace them. And keep your notebook in your storage box. Bear in mind you can also do this by creating files and folders on your computer.

Tip #8. Have you ever been carded? 3 x 5s, that is…

As you prepare to write your outline, your mind will be flooded with images of your characters in action and ideas for scenes. Take some 3 x 5 cards. On each card make a note of:

1. The setting or place where the scene will occur (the San Diego Zoo, the narthex of the cathedral, the amusement park).
2. The time (day or night, a.m., p.m., date).
3. The viewpoint character for this scene.
4. A two or three sentence summary of the action that takes place in this scene.

Once you have a stack of these 3 x 5s filled out, place them in chronological order. Voila! You've just about finished plotting your novel!

If you want to take this one step further, purchase colored cards. Get pink, green, blue and yellow. Transfer the information from above onto pink cards for love scenes, green for action, yellow for scenes mostly composed of conversation or internal dialogue and blue for pivotal scenes that significantly advance the plot.

Spread the completed cards out on the table or the carpet and you can tell at a glance if you have too many action scenes lumped together or too many "talking heads".

Although a tad gimmicky, this can help you make sure that your plot moves forward at a good pace and that you have variety in the placement of your scenes.

An example: The following are scenes outlined for a novel-in progress entitled *Deadly Visions* (which has since been published).

Chapter One: Scene One
Date/Time: Thursday, June 1, 2003—4 p.m.
POV character: Hap Forrester
Place: Dining room of Tarpon Inn
What happens: As the book opens, Hap Forrester is supervising an interior decorator who is hanging and adjusting new draperies in the hotel's dining room. She falls from the ladder. Hap is already upset because he is expecting Felicity, his 10-year-old daughter, to arrive momentarily and he hasn't seen her for more than a year (he's divorced) and because he and the Inn have been plagued by a series of accidents. Now the designer, a woman he respects and likes, has been seriously injured.

Chapter Two, Scene One
Date/Time: Same day, around 5:30 p.m.
POV character: Felicity Forrester
Place: Launch bringing Felicity to Tarpon Inn
What happens: Felicity experiences a bumpy ride across the bay to Useffa Island where Tarpon Inn is located. She arrives to see the injured interior designer being taken to the hospital on the mainland. She is met by her father who welcomes her although she is very uncomfortable with him. One of the first staff members Felicity meets is Markuss Harper, the night clerk. He is black, given second sight and foresees difficult times ahead for Felicity although he doesn't tell her. She just notices he looks troubled.

Tip #9. Time must march on—make your own calendar.

Credibility is essential to the fiction writer. If you don't create a sense of reality or authenticity, you lose your readers. It's that simple.

So how do you develop the element of authenticity?

One way is by paying attention to detail and time is one of those details.

Your novel must have a time line; that is, it must begin and end on specific dates. You do not need to hit your reader over the head with these dates; you need not emphasize the date by placing it at the beginning of each chapter. You must, however, know for yourself when the book begins and ends and refer to time sporadically.

And the book must move forward in time. Use flashbacks sparingly and keep them short. Unless skillfully done, flashbacks can confuse the reader and slow the plot. More on flashbacks in Chapter 8.

While you're still planning, figure out how much time your book spans and decide on a starting date for the first scene or prolog. Then, make your own calendar drawing good-sized boxes for each date so that you have room to write.

Next, refer to your 3 x 5 cards and make notes of the action and scenes on the calendar. You can also make note of the exact dates on the 3 x 5 cards.

You'll find that by creating your own calendar, you have a good overview of your plot and your pace. You'll also find you unconsciously write with your timeline in mind and this helps develop your book's credibility.

There's another bonus to working with a calendar. By knowing the actual date, you can do research and include actual historical events in your calendar. If, for example, you are using your hometown as an interesting, credible backdrop, you can refer to copies of your hometown newspaper at your library and use actual events as a backdrop for your scenes. This is an excellent way to create the sense of authenticity.

You must also remember that the characters in your novels observe holidays. Is there a community in the United States that does not observe Halloween or Thanksgiving or the Fourth of July, for instance? Of course not, and if your characters ignore these, you lose credibility. Your calendar can serve as a reminder because sometimes we can get so caught up in our own plot, we forget what was happening in the real world.

You can also use time and your calendar to artificially generate and superimpose suspense. Set a deadline—an actual date or time—for some showdown, some crisis that leads to the climax of your book. Then as each day passes, your readers will grow more and more concerned for the welfare of your well-drawn characters.

One technique writers use is to begin each chapter with either the date or, if the time in the novel is really compressed, with the hour. This might not work for you and your book, but it is an option. So think about it…

On the next page is a partial calendar prepared for a novel in progress:

September, 2002						
Sunday	**Monday**	**Tuesday**	**Wednesday**	**Thursday**	**Friday**	**Saturday**
1	2 Corey reports to her new job.	3	4 Linda McDaniel is murdered; Corey is assigned to cover murder, write story.	5	6	7
8	9	10 Corey covers a fire at the cola plant and is hit on the head, sent to hospital.	11	12	13	14
15	16	17	18	19	20	21
22	23	24	25	26	27	28 Corey is attacked by killer in her home because she won't stop investigation; killer dies.
29	30	**Notes:** Obviously, you'll have more entries, but this will give you an idea. You can also use this space for notes of information you need to include, corrections, and data you need to research. (Taken from Prudy Taylor Board's calendar for *Murder a la Carte*, also previously published.)				

Tip #10. Still another timely tip.

By placing your action against a real calendar, you can use the backdrop of actual news events and holidays to create a sense of excitement and add color to your book. For example, if part of your novel's action falls in November, say November 22, 2013 for our purposes, you'll include some news coverage of the 50th anniversary of President John F. Kennedy's assassination. And sometimes by doing a little research, you may uncover an interesting or relatively obscure holiday that would make a colorful backdrop for a scene. St. Michael's Feast Day, for example. Or National Pickle Week.

Tip #11. Forget the dog! If you have a computer, the Internet is your new best friend. (If you don't have a computer, the reference librarian can be your salvation.)

First: If you have a computer and most of us do these days, you're not only in touch with worlds of information, you're no longer alone. Chat groups, especially those for, by and with writers, offer places to vent, (discreetly, please—you never know who's online), access to sources of information and research data and, depending on the publisher or agent, even access to guidelines and submissions.

You'll find a list of websites you should check out in Tip 124, but here, let's talk briefly about two warnings. Alert No. 1: As you may already know, professional researchers and journalists strive for three sources for the same information. Before using any research data, try to verify it by at least two, preferably three, independent sources. Alert No. 2: Chatting on the Internet can become a habit and time consuming. Make sure when you're on the Internet, you keep your priorities simple: Writing comes first!

Second: Get to know the local librarian who commands the reference desk. That person can be absolutely invaluable and save you untold hours. Even if you don't know the reference librarian personally, chances are good you can get splendid cooperation----even over the telephone. Keep a couple things in mind: Avoid a hunting expedition. Go through your notes before you call and pinpoint precisely the information you need. Be explicit when you talk to the librarian. Share the information you already have. This may be of help to him or her in the quest to locate your data.

Third: Be sure to tell the librarian that you're a writer working on a novel. Librarians love to help writers—after all, without us, where would they be?

Tip #12. Sum up—before you begin.

Before you set pen to paper or fingers to your computer's keyboard, reduce your novel's plot and premise to a two-sentence summary. Print it in big letters and post it on the card on which you've posted your novel's title and potential completion date so you can see it every time you sit down to write. Focusing this narrowly on the plot and premise will help you in your planning and writing. It will also keep you on target as you write.

Tip #13. First (w)rites needn't be fatal.

When you're starting, give yourself a break. Accept that it's going to take time to get into the heart of the book, to feel empathy for the characters and to get the plot rolling at a good pace. So don't expect perfection. If you can't think of the exact word, leave a blank. If you can't remember how to spell a word, guess. If your punctuation is lousy, that's okay, too. You'll have time to make it right as you progress with the manuscript.

The important thing is to get it out of your head and on the page. It's not a good idea for most writers, however, to write a really sloppy first draft that's going to require major rewrites. To most novelists, the two most beautiful words in the English language are not I do but The End. You can easily get discouraged if you must do four or five major rewrites.

A better way is to plan ahead and make each chapter the best you can so that when you're finished with the first draft, you have only a minor clean-up job staring you in the face.

The preceding blanks should give you enough to get a good start, perhaps even chart your entire book depending on its length. One reminder: Something must happen in every scene. People sitting around talking is not action; telephone conversations are not action. People must move, act—both physically, mentally and emotionally—and react. They cannot simply talk!

PENCIL SHARPENER: Take one of your favorite books, ideally it will be similar to the one you are writing. Re-read it and, on the lines below outline the first three or four chapters using the techniques you learned earlier in this chapter.

CHAPTER 2: PLOTTING IS A ROAD MAP WITH DETOURS

Three magic words apply when it comes to plotting; Conflict, complication and resolution. But first, let's break plot into the two basic types. The first is character driven. In a character-driven plot, the writer's emphasis is more on why things happen than on what happens. And, in character-driven plot, the complications and conflicts arise from the dominant character traits of the protagonist and other major characters. Most literary fiction is based on character-driven plots.

The second is action driven. In this type of plot, the reader is more interested in what usually happens than why it happens. The emphasis is on the action. If it's a murder mystery, the focus is usually on the murderer's gory methods of murder and on the ways the murder is solved rather than why the murder was committed in the first place or why the victim turned out to be the victim. In the action-driven plot, each complication hinders or slows the protagonist in achieving his or her main goal which is either surviving or solving the murder or both. Most genre novels—westerns, mysteries, science fiction, fantasy, men's action, horror—are based on action-driven plots. (Well-written fiction always contains well drawn characters; it's a matter of emphasis.)

Next, let's consider the conflict which constitutes your main storyline. The four basic conflicts are well known, but bear repeating not only because they can be used as the foundation for themes, but also because you've perhaps never broken them into subgroups. The following is a partial list, but if you break these down, you'll see the ideas, the major conflicts, are really limitless. First, the four:

1. **Human against Human:** One person wants something another person has—an object, the love of someone, a job. Or two or more people vie to possess the same object or person. Or to achieve the same goal—two people want the same role in a movie, the same award, the same promotion. A variation is when one person wants to accomplish a goal while another is determined to prevent that man or woman from accomplishing it.

2. **Human against Nature:** Your protagonist must battle the forces of nature to survive or succeed. Your protagonist is caught in a hurricane, a tornado, a plague-wracked city.

3. **Human against God or Fate:** Bad breaks, quirks of coincidence and/or fate, irrational timing strike all of us. These impact fictional characters as well. You'll hear negative comments about the use of coincidence in fiction, but coincidences can be very useful as long as you use them to set up a conflict and don't rely on them to resolve the major conflict. The protagonist must solve his or her own problems.

While we're talking about plotting, you should learn the term *deus ex machina*. A staple of ancient Grecian drama, *deus ex machina* is a situation where the major conflict is literally resolved by gods who descend from the skies in machines. Remember the melodrama where the nasty, mustache twirling landlord is going to throw poor Mary out because she's behind in the mortgage payments? At the last moment when Mary is standing in the snow with her meager belongings heaped at her feet, a check arrives from her grandmother saving the day. *Deus ex machina*. This might have worked centuries ago, but current readers will not accept this. Your protagonist can receive advice and assistance, but when the final confrontation arrives he or she must solve the problem.

4. **Human against Himself**: The idea that we are our own worst enemies is not new, but it can be the basis for a good story. Your character's greed, impatience, indifference or inappropriate generosity, for example, creates the conflict and complications your protagonist must resolve.

Next the subgroups. If you further break down these four conflicts, you see what a wonderful range of conflicts is available: **Human against Human** translates into man against woman; man against child; man or men against women; woman against woman, against a man, against all men, against a child, against all children, earthlings against Martians. And each changes the elements of conflict. Child against child, against adults, old against young, group against group.

When you think about **Human against Human**, you find it rife with opportunity for you are not merely dealing with one human competing against another, you are given the opportunity of pitting one human against society's mores, against laws and government, against customs, traditions, moral codes, religious beliefs.

When you think in terms of **Human against Nature**, it translates into men, women and/or children battling to survive flood, drought, tornadoes, hurricanes, the sea, mountains, rivers, deserts, earthquakes, animals, or terrorist attacks. Diseases and plagues. Feral housecats. And don't forget that the incredible scientific advances made in recent years provides a host of new possibilities— engineered genes going awry, manipulated DNA.

In the category of **Human against God and Fate**, other elements come into play including human against ghosts, against psychic phenomena, against outer space, human against aliens.

Human against Self is where the character-driven novel comes into its own because this involves not only the acts one commits, but also the conscience one has that governs one's reactions to those acts. Or the major conflict can stem from an act of omission, the act a character or protagonist does not commit, that he or she knows he should have. It can involve the juxtaposition of one set of values against another. The training and habits from the past, as opposed to the demands of the future. The demands of the heart superimposed against the demands of the mind. The possibilities—given the infinite variety of character traits, the intricacy of their linking within human beings—are limitless.

Conflict must be about significant issues.

Beginning writers sometimes err in that the conflict they present is neither significant nor major. If you are too kind hearted, too compassionate, if you can't give your protagonist dire problems, you probably should be writing the gentler cozy mysteries. Even then, the conflicts must exist, but are written sans gore and with a lighter touch. Your hero or your heroine must stand to gain or lose something of tremendous value. The characters must have something vitally important at stake. And, in order to have a story worth telling, your major conflict cannot have a simple solution.

For example, let's say your heroine is an impoverished teenager asked by the high school hunk to be his prom date. She has no gown and is desperate. On the face of it, that is not significant enough to carry an entire novel because she has choices and easy solutions. Her parents can do without to get her gown (not good—because she is not solving her own problem), she can buy the material and her mother can make her gown, she can borrow a gown from a friend or she can get a job and work to save money.

Now if all of these options fail and she is driven to try to steal a gown and is thus launched on a life of crime, you may have something albeit a little over the top In other words, both the conflict and the consequences must be life altering.

Tip #14. Don't use too many ingredients in your stewplot—this is one of those times when less is better.

When you plot your novel—especially your first—consider limiting yourself to one major conflict. This can be a conflict, for example, between your protagonist and your villain or villains, a conflict between a protagonist and an obstacle such as his conscience, or the conflict between a protagonist and a looming, lurking natural disaster. As you become more experienced, you will be better able to handle multiple plot lines.

If you have only your major storyline, your novel may lack complexity and interest, but don't panic! To remedy this problem, use conflicts involving your secondary characters as minor conflicts and subplots. In a novel published some years ago and made into a movie entitled "The Flight of the Phoenix," the major conflict was the plane wreck and the survival of these men in the desert—Human against Nature. The depth, the richness, the texture of that story came from the minor conflicts between the men that occurred as they tried to resolve the major conflict—their ultimate survival. The conflicts surfaced as they tried to decide what to do. The ways the men faced their individual and collective jeopardies not only lent suspense, but revealed character as well as providing complications.

Along the road to the denouement or the plot resolution, your protagonist must face the second element of plotting—complications. These are nothing more than the obstacles that arise to make it more difficult for the hero or heroine to resolve the main conflict. The third element of plotting—the resolution—enters the scene here because as you introduce each complication, your characters must attempt to resolve it. Your character does not have to successfully resolve each complication, but must try.

Let's say, for example, you have placed your protagonist in a life-threatening or life-altering situation at the very beginning of the book. (Good for you!) If, by the end of chapter one, your hero has resolved the major conflict, if she has gone through the battle or the test and has resolved it, your book is over. So as you plot this book, think in terms of creating a series of complications that gradually escalate in significance and severity as the protagonist attempts to resolve the major problem.

When you are seeking complications to muddy your protagonist's path, where do you look? One place is real life. We all face minor complications every day of our lives. We oversleep. We're fifteen minutes late to work. In a novel, however, you exaggerate the consequences.

Your hero is having serious financial problems. He also habitually oversleeps. As your book opens, your protagonist goes in to work and he is fifteen minutes late. He loses his job. Or his life is pretty much a mess and he is late for a tennis date Saturday morning. His girlfriend greets him saying, "I warned you that if you were late one more time, Buster, you'd be history!" And he's madly in love with her, and must have her or die. The major conflict here is the financial difficulty or that he is losing the only woman he could ever love; the fact that he is late is a complication.

Complications move the plot forward.

Another place to look for complications is the world in which your characters live. If your hero is a lawyer, the complications may arise from the law, from his law practice, his relationships with his clients, co-workers and the staff in the courtroom. If she's a cop, complications may be found in her social life, her relationships with her superiors, her peers, the people on the streets, her family.

Your complications must be exaggerated yet always believable. You accomplish this when they are drawn from and based on real life. And again, the complications must grow in seriousness as your book progresses. This creates the growing suspense and intensity. Your protagonist has financial problems. He loses his job. That's bad. He starts drinking. That's bad. Then he loses his home. That's worse. And his car. Now he doesn't even have transportation to look for work. He and his wife move in with his family. He and his wife argue and she takes the children and leaves. The problems he faces have grown steadily worse—some because of his own actions, some because of his wife's, some because he's short of money. The stakes grow even higher for the protagonist—and the reader—as each complication arises.

At this point in your planning, you should be working on your book's pace. As a writer, your goal should be to write a book so engrossing (so meaningful if you strive for mainstream or literary), so captivating that once the readers read your first scintillating paragraph they cannot put your book down. When you think back on books you've cherished and remembered, weren't these the books where the writer hooked you on the first page and didn't let go? You didn't care if you had to stay up till dawn, if you had to lie in bed reading with your legs crossed, or if the house was burning down around you. You had to finish that book, had to see what was going to happen next.

Begin with that goal in mind and work toward it as diligently and intelligently as you can. Not only will your writing be immensely better, you stand a much better chance of reaching the best seller list.

Pacing is not accidental. It doesn't just happen. You create your pace while you are planning your plot. And you design it like a blueprint. There are a number of ways that you establish a brisk, forward-moving pace.

One important thing to remember in planning your pacing is that you must vary both the length and the emotional color and content of the individual scenes. For example, if you have a great deal of physical action in a book, you don't want to lump all these physical scenes together. This becomes tedious. Vary scenes of physical action with kinder, gentler scenes as a contrast. Contrast those emotional scenes with more cerebral scenes in which the character talks or thinks. Strive for that variety.

Remember: A reader cannot comfortably maintain an intense emotional reaction over a long period of time. That's why when you have a book full of fearsome happenings, you will find that a graphically violent scene may be followed by a loving or humorous scene to give the reader a break. This variety also establishes pace.

Just be sure you don't fall into a set pattern. Physical scene, cerebral scene, love scene, talky scene, physical scene, cerebral scene, love scene, talky scene. Avoiding a pattern will help you avoid being predictable.

Another way to keep the pace brisk is by making sure that you brutally slash every single word that doesn't earn its keep. Unnecessary words slow the reader's eyes as they move physically across the page and the reader correlates that slower reading pace with the pace of the novel.

Consider energizing the pace and heightening the suspense by superimposing a deadline—a ticking clock. A wonderful example of that is a film by Russell Crouse entitled "D.O.A." At the very beginning of the film, the hero stumbles into the police station and says, "I have come to report a murder." The hardened, cynical homicide detective says, "Whose murder?" and the hero responds, "Mine." We learn he has been poisoned and has only twenty-four hours to live. We travel with him as he discovers the identity of his murderer and foils his plan within that deadline before dying.

You can use that same mechanical deadline. As mentioned in Tip 9, set any sort of deadline. It doesn't have to be a murder mystery. Take a mainstream novel where a couple is to be married at three o'clock on Saturday and at two p.m. Friday afternoon, the bridegroom discovers his bride-to-be in bed with another man. If you have the superimposed deadline of three o'clock, you create immediate suspense. The reader is asking will they or won't they get married? Or you can have a mother with a child who is ill. The medicine to treat the child's rare disease is in a city at a far distance. The child has only hours to live. Can the doctors get the medicine to the child in time?

Be aware that when you are working on a plot, it develops along a rather predictable framework. The major plot is established; the first complication appears; a partial resolution to the complication eases the pressure. Then the next complication occurs.

Don't worry. While the basic structure may be predictable, the complications and characters themselves won't be—that's where your creativity comes to play.

How can you avoid predictability? By really knowing your characters, by letting them decide how they're going to resolve the complications or throw roadblocks in the paths of other characters. Become intimate with your characters, look to their landscape and the people around them, then stay out of the way.

Tip #15. Bulk up your novel with dramatic muscle; don't pad it with words.

If you are ever approached by an editor to expand your book, don't add words. Add scenes featuring your protagonist. Always remember that these additional scenes must serve a purpose— they must include action which moves the plot forward. They cannot be added just to lengthen your book. If adding scenes doesn't work, develop subplots involving the secondary characters who surround your protagonist. Give them dreams, goals and story lines of their own.

Within the framework of a novel's plot, there will and must be moments of revelation and truth as the characters work toward achieving their goals. These are the moments when the characters gain insight into themselves or when they garner new information about the forces arrayed against them.

But in any novel, there must be one moment of truth that supersedes all the others. This is the scene where the protagonist comes to understand for the first time all the ramifications of the real problem he or she must face.

At this point in a character-driven plot, your protagonist comes to honestly evaluate himself or herself and makes the decision that resolves the plot. The protagonist comes to realize, "I have been a selfish boor." Or "I have been sloppy in my relationships." Or "I have been too trusting." He recognizes his major character flaw and makes the decision at that point in time that solves the problem or else he doesn't and suffers the consequences.

In the action driven novel, this is the moment of insight and inspiration when the protagonist realizes what he can do to resolve the problem. The hero's in a burning warehouse. He doesn't know how he's going to get out, but in the previous scenes you have planted that there is a boarded up trap door and the hero either finds it or remembers it. He finds a hammer, pries the boards away, uncovers the trap door and escapes. This is the moment when all the storylines come together, when the character realizes what he must do to save himself, or resolve the problem.

Tip #16. The shortest distance between two points is not a straight line when you're plotting.

You cannot make it too easy for your characters to realize their dreams or achieve their goals. Think of plotting as trying to climb a mountain while wearing ordinary shoes as opposed to proper gear. Your character progresses a hundred feet and things are looking good. Then he slips and slides back 20 feet. He pulls himself together and starts again. This time he progresses 150 feet, but is stopped when the path he's been following ends and he must backtrack and start from another vantage point.

If you prefer, think of your plot as having a beginning and an ending point, then think of the section in between as having a series of zigs and zags. Each obstacle or complication is represented by a zig; each resolution of the complication is represented by a zag. If you have a straight line from beginning to end, a straight line between need and desire and the accomplishment of that goal, you have no conflict, no complication, and, therefore, no story.

Tip #17. Are you an author in search of a plotting shed?

The classics in the library might qualify as a source, a metaphorical shed containing all the basic conflicts, plus truly good plots are all around us. In the newspaper—an article about political corruption (and Heaven knows there is enough of that), or about a crooked cop, or a revenge killing, or the librarian who works as an exotic dancer at night. The six o'clock news…documentaries… conversations overheard at the laundromat or the beauty parlor or the airport.

Plots and fascinating characters are abundant. We need only sensitize ourselves to them. And, oh, those Greeks! And we're not talking Aristotle Onassis or Maria Callas, although their lives were certainly fascinating. We're talking about the big guys—Zeus and his crowd. The plots the Greeks used in developing their mythology are as timely—if appropriately updated—as they were then. And certainly look at the other classics. What is "West Side Story," but a contemporary version of *Romeo and Juliet*? And how many times has *Pygmalion* been updated?

Tip #18. Everybody has a dream—a/k/a motivation.

Think of motivation as the key you slip into your novel's ignition. Motivation is what gets your characters off their rear ends and into action.

Let each character want something desperately. Or be desperately afraid of something that might, probably will happen. Then your character's motivation is to avoid it. Make sure complications and problems and delays arise. Immediately. Remember this as well. Your characters don't have to want positive things—they can want revenge, or to keep someone else from accomplishing or acquiring something. It's good plotting when two characters want the same thing—the same girl, the same job, the same jewel. That creates conflict and you want conflict.

Remember: Without conflict, you have no story because nothing happens.

Tip #19. Games people play—double dealing, deception. Secrets are vital to your plot.

Everybody's got at least one secret—one hidden event or act or piece of knowledge they don't want the rest of the world to know. Your characters are people, aren't they? Give them secrets. When you're doing your initial planning, give each character a secret he or she doesn't want revealed. And then let the other characters figure out what that secret is. And react to it once it's revealed.

Remember: Characters don't always tell one another the truth any more than people do. And it's quite often the lies they tell that lead to the complications.

Remember, two: Characters don't always do what they say they are going to do. Or they do something entirely different from what they've said they're going to do. This type of deception is very valuable to the plotter.

Tip #20. Here's a Q tip for your endings.

Think of the letter Q when you're planning the ending of your novel. The plot should circle back to the beginning for unity. You can accomplish this in a myriad of ways—the more original the better, of course, but common ways are to have it the same season as when the novel began, or maybe have the book end in the setting where it began, or maybe the characters are doing the same thing. Or perhaps using the same symbol.

Naturally, a lot has happened since the book began, but this completed circle, this element common to the beginning creates a sense of completion that is very satisfying to the reader.

And the little fillip or tail of the Q? That's an important element of the plot as well. Just when the reader is mentally enjoying the nicely organized ending in which you've answered all his questions, filled all the loopholes and appropriately rewarded your characters, throw in a kicker. Something unexpected. This, too, is something you must consider when you're planning your book because it must not seem contrived. It must grow out of decisions or actions of your characters or the plot.

Save one last plot thread and make it a knot as opposed to a bow!

PENCIL SHARPENER #1: Perhaps the best text on plotting ever created is any novel by Sidney Sheldon. *Rage of Angels* is excellent. But remember to read it as a writer, not a reader. Figure out why you can never put one of his books down. Pay attention to the way he ends his chapters, structures his scenes. Take the time to do an outline of one of his books and you'll understand the realities, not the theories, of plotting. Here's a hint: Look for the surprises. In every chapter you'll find something unexpected. That's known as a plot turn. Look for them. Plan for them.

PENCIL SHARPENER #2: Take three best sellers you've enjoyed reading and go through each chapter by chapter and scene by scene for at least the first ten chapters and the last three. Analyze each scene: Who is the point of view character, where does the scene take place, how much time has elapsed since the previous scene and, of course, summarize the action of the scene in a sentence or two. If you really want to write a good, saleable novel, learn from the best.

Then take the next step. Evaluate each scene to determine whether it's cerebral in that it's mostly in one character's thoughts, emotional, physical or mostly dialogue. See if you can discover a pattern. Is the author predictable? Or are you constantly surprised? As a reader, which do you prefer? Why?

NOTES:_____

_____

_____

_____

_____

_____

_____

_____

_____

_____

_____

_____

_____

_____

_____

_____

_____

_____

_____

_____

_____

_____

_____

_____

_____

_____

_____

_____

CHAPTER 3: PEOPLING YOUR PAGES

In creating characters for your novels, you have four primary goals:

Goal 1: Make your people unique and interesting. This means that if your heroine is going to be a secretary or a housewife, she has to be a very interesting secretary or housewife. She must have an interesting past, engrossing relationships and hobbies, admirable goals and intriguing ideas and outlooks on life. And you must know her extremely well. If your hero works in an office or a bank, the same applies to him.

To create the requisite uniqueness, however, you must look beyond the label or the role. Take the private detective. We've had hundreds, probably thousands of private detectives as heroes of novels. The ones who've made an indelible image on our lives are the ones who are unique. Think about Sherlock Holmes. Arthur Conan Doyle gave him flaws, an ego, the use of cocaine to assuage his sense of boredom; he gave him an incredible mind, a love of music, a sense of humor. Doyle created a unique character. That's what you must strive to do.

Goal 2: Be sure your characters have motivations for their actions, opinions and decisions and that the reader understands these motives. Let's say you establish a character who has a tremendous drive for success. You need to let the reader know why success is so important to this character so the reader can accept not only this character's tremendous ambition, but the lengths to which the character will go for success. You want to give the villain, the hero, the heroine, even the secondary characters in your subplots reasons for doing what they are doing. If you don't, if your characters just do what they are told, you have created puppets or caricatures, not believable characters.

Goal 3: And one of the most important is to make your characters believable. One of the tools you have in creating believable characters is the selective use of specific details and we'll talk about that a little later in more detail.

And finally, **Goal 4:** Create characters who will evoke emotional responses from your readers. Your reader cannot be indifferent to the hero, the heroine and the villain, which means you need to spend ample time creating these characters as well-rounded and lifelike. Your protagonist must have character attributes that render him likeable and admirable. Ask yourself what traits you can give the villain that will make him truly heinous, yet someone the reader can related to. If you don't take the time to create a background for your characters, if you don't invest this time, your characters will be one-dimensional.

It's important to be aware, especially in commercial fiction, that your hero or your heroine cannot be either a loser or a wimp. Readers want to read about and relate to winners. Furthermore, you can no longer develop the heroine as a character who, at the climax of the book, is rescued by the hero. The heroine of today must rescue herself. She must figure out the solution to her problem on her own. She can have help, but readers of today do not want to read about helpless females.

At the same time, you must not make your heroine a superwoman. When you do that, you reduce your heroine to a caricature and readers won't relate to her.

Remember: While you are creating this heroine as a strong independent, decisive woman, she must have quirks and flaws, compassion and caring—soft spots.

To find the quirks and flaws you need, look to the weaknesses that create problems for the people around you. You find them in your family, your close friends and co-workers—and yourself. You find them in your enemies. You find them in the conversations you hear while in the supermarket. You find them in real life.

One of my best friends is a feature writer for a daily newspaper and not too long ago she was visiting from out-of-town and we went to the movies. She drove and when we came out to get into her car, I saw that her left front fender was dented. I didn't say a word. When she drives, she gets so involved in conversation that she doesn't watch where she's going and has fender benders all the time. She would make a delightful character, although it would be important to make certain either that she cannot recognize herself or that she knows what I'm doing and gives her permission.

Don't worry. In the process of creating interesting characters that engage the reader's emotions, you will simultaneously create believable characters. The two processes work together. It's an extremely esoteric example of serendipity.

Don't make the mistake of shortchanging your bad guys. Sometimes as writers we tend to neglect our villains. We create them as phantoms or we just don't let them on stage too often. There are several reasons for this. We may not want to spend time with vicious, selfish characters. Or perhaps they are so evil, such as serial murderers, that we just don't want to visit the grief they create. Or we may feel that, as decent human beings ourselves, we don't know that much about evil. Those excuses won't wash if you want to be a successful writer.

Begin by thinking of your villain as a human being and, if it helps, give him or her some positive attributes first. Then, once the villain is real to you, add the bad (or good) stuff that makes him memorable.

This exercise will do double duty. Your villain must also be carefully crafted because he or she must also be believable. If you create a totally villainous villain, the reader will not believe the character because everyone knows there is some measure of good in all of us. Also, an entirely evil villain would be so repulsive that the reader would not want to spend three or four hundred pages of his or her reading time with this person.

Why must a villain be believable, you ask? (I'm glad you asked!) It's because of that unspoken, unwritten contract that exists between the reader and the writer first described by Samuel Coleridge Taylor as "the willing suspension of disbelief." For example, although readers know vampires do not exist, they will agree to believe in vampires while they read your book. In other words, they will willingly suspend their disbelief until they have finished reading. Your part of the bargain is to do your best to make vampires and their world as believable as possible.

How do you create a believable villain?

Much the same way you create your hero. Just a little bit of the reverse in that whereas you give the hero some flaws to make him less than superman, you give the villain some good qualities. When you're in the process of creating a villain, work through his background as thoroughly as the hero's.

Let the villain have a mother he worships, or a wife, son or daughter. A cause he believes in strongly. Let him have a pet he adores. Let him have positive traits. While the reader may not be able to pull for the villain to be victorious, a skillful writer can create for the reader a dichotic concern.

On the one hand, the reader experiences dismay that the villain is getting into more and more trouble and can't win, yet cheering for the hero to be sure that he, the hero, does win.

The hero and the villain both must have obvious and believable goals. They should be almost equally matched in intelligence and power. They should each have something of vital importance to win or lose. They should be worthy adversaries for one another. If they are equally matched, you are able to create more suspense, because in one complication the hero wins, and in the second, the villain wins. The balance of power constantly shifts and the reader is never completely sure who will win.

The key to creating believable characters is to take your time. Spend time with them. Create fully detailed backgrounds for each of your major characters.

Consider four areas: 1. Your character's heredity, his ancestry, his roots, his body and appearance. 2. Your character's surroundings, the milieu in which he lives and operates. 3. Your character's life experiences. 4. Your character's ideas and beliefs.

Your character's inherited traits, physical and mental, are going to impact his life and his reactions to his life. Obviously your character is going to have a body, unless you are doing something incredibly clever in science fiction or fantasy. And this body, its shape, height, physical fitness and strength, weight, will affect the way that character moves through the world and perceives himself or herself.

Beyond that, your character will have inherited certain traits. Perhaps the way a character handles stress. For example, a young woman who works in an office is a tiny, tiny little thing. She's not quite five feet tall and weighs about ninety-eight pounds, and whenever stress builds she gets a horrendous stomachache. There's her boss, an overweight bachelor with an attitude. When he feels stress, his laws and shoulders tighten and he gets a backache. It's a combination of heredity, personality, and body build.

Timidity, enthusiasm for taking risks or a reluctance to do so, these are also affected by social heredity, and the development of a family over more than one generation. It's very important when you are creating your characters that you think not only in terms of the characters as they are today but how they were as they grew up. Be aware and sensitive to the fact that a character's age, sex and health will also affect the way he lives in his body, the way he moves.

As a writer, look at people in terms of decades, or portions of their life. The twenty-year-olds today, especially in their middle twenties, react to things very differently from teenagers. People in their twenties today are health conscious, careful about what they eat, careful to work out. People in their sixties and seventies are a different generation. Physical fitness isn't as important to them. They are inclined to drink more. If they grew up in the sixties, they have a different attitude toward drugs and booze and may prefer grass.

Obviously the physical reactions of the generations are very different. An eighteen-year-old watching TV in a living room will wait for a commercial break then get up, run to the kitchen to get a can of soda, sit back down, make a quick phone call or go get something else, whereas the fifty-year-old will sit there, use the remote control, wait for the commercial break, call his or her significant other to bring a drink. He'll do two or three things at once because he is more conscious of conserving energy.

Your best source is watching people, but watch them as a writer. Sensitize yourself to observe all of life as a writer.

The next area you need to carefully consider is each character's surroundings because these also mold your character. A heroine who grows up in New Orleans will be different from one who grows up in Brooklyn. A hero who grows up in Miami will have a different approach to life than one who grows up in Punta Gorda, a small town on the west coast of Florida.

Their language will be different, their frame of reference, the significant events of their lives will be different. A villain growing up in New Orleans might go down to that wonderful Café du Monde in the French Quarter on a Saturday morning for coffee and beignets. Pronounced "ben-YAYS," these are the rectangular doughnuts—no holes—served fresh and hot 24/7 in New Orleans. On the other hand, when growing up in Old Miami, the villain might have gone to Wolfie's for a hot pastrami sandwich on rye with a Kosher dill pickle.

You must also remember that within the cities there are different neighborhoods. If your character grows up in an ethnic neighborhood, the values of that society will be his values, they will affect him. The holidays, the festivals in that community, these will be parts of his background that you may draw on to create him. The character of the neighborhood will impact your character as well. For example, a hero who lives in a golf course community in Florida will be different from a hero that grows up in a slum section, or a hero who lives in a modest neighborhood of blue-collar Americans.

In short: when you are creating your character, you need to know a lot more than height, weight, hair and eye colors.

The other category is the character's life experiences. Think about those personal experiences and relationships with old girlfriends or those personal experiences and relationships with ex-wives and ex-husbands and specific events that have had a lasting impact on the way that character developed into an adult human being. Family arguments. Break-ups. Divorces. Successes. They make us who we are and that works for characters as well.

Think about job experiences. Not just the kind of work the character does, but how does he get along with his boss? Did he move up in that business or did he leave? Arguments he might have had with his boss. Maybe he has a problem with authority figures, or maybe he was fired one time because it was wrongly assumed he had stolen something. The traumatic experiences, the deaths, the devastations, the failures as well as the successes. (These secondary characters—ex-wives, old boyfriends, etc.—can also be wonderful sources of subplots.)

Chart your character's life so that you understand the major experiences the character has had and how those experiences have affected him. And you need to give thought as well to what the character learned from each experience or didn't learn and how the character reacted.

The next category is your character's ideas and beliefs. What are this character's beliefs that have shaped him or her? Is he an anti-Republican, a strong Democrat? Is she pro-life? Is he opposed to the use of animals in medical research? Does this person have an idea that all women are not too bright, to be patted on the head and put in the corner? Does this woman think that all men are unreliable, untruthful and not to be trusted? What are the causes your character believes in and works for or against.

These are important because they tell you a great deal about your characters. Maybe you can do something interesting with a point in the character's life when she was very impressionable and she was exposed to a group or a person who opened her mind, or taught her to think about life in a different way. Perhaps this could be one of those life experiences that was significant.

Your character's background not only tells you why the character does what he does, it may also tell you why he doesn't do something else—the acts he fails to commit, the things he decides not to do.

You also need to surround your characters with specifics. The clothes your characters wear, things they choose to collect, the things they choose to discard, their attitudes toward money, toward their cars.

Don't ignore that word specific. If there is a painting on the wall, it's probably not a Rousseau. How many of our characters can afford Rousseau? But it might be a painting by Paul Billie, a Seminole artist, as opposed to just an unnamed Indian. If your character has a pet, the pet has a name, the pet has an appearance and, again, the kind of pet your character has will tell you a lot about the character. These elements are very important as you build the background against which your character operates.

Know where your character lives, and not just that he lives in San Francisco or New Orleans or Miami. Your character lives at 1710 SW Eighth Street or 339 Maple Avenue. You must know that your character lives not just in a rooming house, but in Ma Appleton's in the back room on the third floor overlooking the backyard with the clothesline. Or that your character has a condominium on the Gulf or the ocean. If your character plays golf your character doesn't just go to the country club, your character goes to a specific country club.

Developing these details of your character's life will help you create the credibility that is so essential in motivating your reader to willingly suspend disbelief.

And don't overlook holidays. A character's reactions to holidays can be very revealing. The publisher of a magazine I once worked for despised and feared Christmas because his younger brother had died in a bad automobile accident on Christmas Day. The man was twenty-five when his brother passed and from that time on until he died in the 1980s, he never again put up a Christmas tree, never bought a Christmas gift, never sent a Christmas card. He avoided all the trappings of holidays. Part of it was grief, part of it was fear and the awareness of his own mortality. (Perhaps he had a "Bah, Humbug!" mentality. In that case, he would be an interesting character, too.)

When you are trying to create the life experiences relevant for the development of your plot, holidays can be very helpful.

Another example: I think of a friend of my late husband's. The friend was Jewish and his children went to public school with Gentile children. As you know, Jewish people don't celebrate Christmas, but the children put so much pressure on the parents that they finally put a Christmas tree on a tea cart. When the grandparents came over, the parents would carefully wheel the tea cart and the Christmas tree into a closet. After the grandparents were gone, they would wheel out the tree again.

Once you are actually writing, you need to be alert to how much character background you're including. To avoid overloading your book with expository material, make every piece of information pass these two tests. **One:** Be sure the reader needs this piece of information in order to understand the plot and/or to believe the character's motivation. **Two:** Be sure it does not slow the story.

If there is background information your reader absolutely must have to understand the plot or the characters, remember that you have several methods for bringing it out to the reader.

First, you can present it as exposition and spread it out. Give the reader a piece of information here and there. Remember Hansel and Gretel and the bread crumbs? Avoid big chunks of exposition whenever possible. You can also give the reader this information by means of the characters' thoughts and dialogue. You have still another very useful tool—point of view—which beginning writers sometimes overlook. Then, too, you can give the reader information about John if you write a scene from Mary's point of view. Let John be seen through Mary's eyes and use Mary's opinions and observations of him to bring him to life for your reader.

Another question you must constantly ask yourself is whether your characters are working and whether they are well drawn. There does come a time when you will know.

There comes a time when your characters take over the story. They are not moving away from the ending you've set for the plot, but they are in charge and may resolve some of the complications in a different manner than you had planned. At this point, you sit back and find yourself saying, "I didn't know that," or "Isn't that interesting," or "How did she think to do that?" That's when you know you've done your job properly and well.

You may also find that as you develop your characters, one becomes more interesting to you than the hero or the heroine. If that's the case, you need to rethink your book. You need to re-evaluate your story line and your hero or heroine.

A friend of mine, a romance writer, started a romance novel at the point where the heroine was about to be married to the hero. As they were exchanging their vows, the villain entered and lied to the priest saying he was already married to the heroine. The villain said he had their children with him. The heroine had never seen them before, but the villain maintained these were their children. The children had been coached and they threw their arms around her skirts and cried, "Mommy, Mommy, you can't marry this man. You're married to Daddy!" As the manuscript progressed, it became obvious the villain was far more fascinating and attractive than the hero. She turned the villain into the hero and the story worked and sold.

Red alert: If you create a character more interesting than your hero or your heroine, you can resolve this problem in several other ways. You can either make that character a secondary character in the present book, playing down his or her story and write another novel featuring this character as the protagonist, or you can just ditch your first idea and rework the outline.

There are two other ways you'll know if your characters are working. If, when you finish the book, you go through a genuine sense of grieving because you miss the characters and you feel as though you've lost friends, that's a clue.

Bottom line: You know your characters have worked when your agent calls or emails and says, "So and So has made an offer on your book."

Tip #21. Create and maintain your cast of characters.

One of the first steps when you start a novel is to create a cast of characters. Begin by making a list. Take a sheet of notebook paper and write each character's name at the top. On this sheet, which you will keep in your notebook or in a file on your PC, make notes of any information that comes to you about that character.

When you begin your outline, you don't have to give your characters names. You can indicate them generically as villain, hero, waitress, etc. You want to take your time selecting names for your characters because names should have as much of an impact on your fictional characters as they do on real folks.

Even though you work with an outline, you may find new characters appearing, sometimes uninvited, in your pages. Be sure to add these to your list.

Tip #22. Foibles, failures and flaws are the writer's friends—describing characters.

Too many times when we write description, we envision our characters as perfect. Boring! Or we focus on the positive aspects of their appearances. However, warts, pimples, a tendency to be plump or skinny, a scar almost invisible to most people, but blatantly obvious to the bearer—these are important elements of description. Why? Because they shape and motivate the character.

In real life, we are often motivated more by our failures (real or otherwise), foibles and flaws than by our triumphs.

When writing description, focus first on those imperfect aspects of your character. Then understand and explain how these anatomical glitches have affected your character. For example, the female character who has a tendency to gain weight will salivate at the sight of fattening foods, but eat her salad and exercise. Or she will indulge, develop guilt-induced heartburn and go jogging. The man with the glass eye, especially if he is vain, may change his entire life's schedule opting to take night jobs. The young woman with the gorgeous body will have an entirely different approach to life.

It's not only important to know that your character has a body and what size it is, you need to know how your character reacts to and lives within that body.

Tip #23. A photograph can be worth a thousand words to a writer.

An important ability worth cultivating is the ability to create pictures in your mind of the person you are currently describing. Failing that, use a photograph. Yes, in your workbook (See Tip #7) you can add a page for a photograph of each character and you can refer back to that photo every time you need to talk to your character or see what she looks like.

Where are you going to get the photos?

Newspapers are an excellent source of interesting faces. Magazines are as well, but not so much the ads as the editorial copy. Sometimes even the artwork. Usually the models in the ads are too perfect to be believable. More than that, their features are often almost nondescript because the reader is supposed to notice the clothing or product.

Another excellent source is the old family album. You'll certainly find real and interesting faces there. Antique and junk shops often have old snapshot albums and photos, too.

Tip #24. Travel with a camera (or a cell phone).

You can develop your own cast of thousands merely by carrying your camera or smart phone when you go on vacation or even short trips. If you see an interesting person, just click that shutter. It's more discreet to shoot the person as part of a crowd, but most people don't notice that you're taking pictures as long as you don't make a big deal out of it. You may not even want the whole person. You may find an interesting mouth, eyebrow or manner of standing.

Learning to really look at people is the first step in learning to describe them.

Tip #25. What's in a name? Lots!

The names you give your characters are important because names have emotional color as well as being identity tags. It's just common sense that you aren't going to call a quick draw hero in a western novel a name commonly perceived as effete such as Percival. You know that. And you're probably not going to name a hooker Chastity or an alcoholic Temperance—unless you're going for irony or satire.

Go beyond the obvious. Be aware of the origin of the names you use and their actual meanings, but think in terms of sound, too. If you want a soft, feminine woman you probably won't name her Vera. Vera is a fine name, but that "V" gives it a hard sound. Sophia. Anna. They have soft sounds.

Spend time selecting names and don't be reluctant to change them in mid-book. Sometimes you have to live with your characters for awhile before they reveal their real names.

And, for heaven's sake, don't be coy or cute. When you first introduce characters to the reader, introduce them by their full names. One of the very first things you should tell the reader is the character's name. If you deliberately hide the character's identity, you must have a very good, solid reason. Otherwise, the reader is going to get irritated. Or equally as bad, the reader will skip ahead to find the character's name out and miss paragraphs of your deathless prose.

Plus, it just makes sense. When you meet someone for the first time, one of the first things you're told is that person's name. Art imitates life!

Tip #26. What's good for baby is good for the writer.

Books used to name babies are excellent sources. They're especially helpful because they give you the derivation of the name and its meaning. Encyclopedias are good sources, especially encyclopedias of fictional characters. But be sure to take a first name from one place and the last name from another.

Obituaries are good sources, but even though a person is dead and can't sue, it's better to combine several names rather than lift one directly from the obit. When you're out of the country, procure a phone book. If you have a novel set in London, it can't hurt to have the names of Londoners for flavor (again, it's best not to lift whole names) as well as the names of important and recognizable streets and businesses.

Tip #27. Avoid confusing your new best friend, your reader.

Once you've named all your characters and made your list, read the list aloud. Make sure you don't have characters with similar sounds. A story with a Joe, a Jack, a Jim and a John or even a

Dom and a Tom or a Gale and a Dale can lead to reader overload and confusion and, finally, to the ultimate reader retribution…putting down your book unread.

Seriously, do double-check your master list of characters to be sure each character's name is so distinct the reader will not confuse one character with another.

Tip #28. Dress your characters for success(ful) characterization.

Fashion designing as a second career? No, you don't have to know that much about clothes, but you do need to know how your characters dress. And their manner of dress can and should be very revealing. (Not anatomically, you understand—unless that's what relevant.) Have a heroine who staples a loose hem? Or a hero who spends more on dry cleaning than groceries? A character who wears only designer labels? Or one who shops second hand shops? And the way your character feels wearing the clothes—confident, overdressed, underdressed, out-of-style—can reveal your character's mood and level of self-esteem.

If you write about historical characters, it's imperative that you become familiar with the clothing of your chosen time period. And if you intend to specialize in one era, it's a good idea to invest in a fashion or costume encyclopedia.

For contemporary novels, you can get great ideas for clothing from women's and men's fashion magazines. And it's a good idea to choose magazines that reflect your character's interests, social and economic status—for instance, if one of your characters drives a motorcycle, check out a motorcycle magazine. Typical housewife? *Family Circle*. Designer clothes? *W*, *Elle*, *Vogue*, *Vanity Fair*.

Specific detail is so important in developing credibility that you must see precisely what each character is wearing in each scene. Again, it's like dressing the characters for a stage play or a movie. Only your characters appear in the theater of your reader's mind so you must tell the reader how they are dressed.

Each time you plan a scene, give some thought to what your characters will wear. Many times clothes are so secondary to the action in a scene that a description would slow things down, but you—the Creative God of Your Empire—will benefit from knowing what they are wearing whether you use that information or not.

Tip #29. When should you use characters from real life?

If you're ever tempted to lift a character directly from the real world, do some research into Marjorie Kinnan Rawlings' life. She did that and not only lost a dear friend, but ended up in court in one of the most celebrated trials in recent literary history. It's usually not advisable. However, fictional characters must resemble real life so there's no reason you can't take certain characteristics from real people.

If you have a friend who's very driven, who walks rapidly, talks rapidly, thinks rapidly, there's no reason you can't base a character on those traits as long as you either tell the person what you're doing or clothe that character in a different body, add a personal background that is very different from the real person's, and give the character a very different name. Actually fictional characters are nearly always inspired by real people.

Sometimes this is easy if you not only change the physical characteristics, but also combine the traits, attitudes, personal histories of several people into one character.

Tip #30. Applying for the job of one of your characters.

This tip is gimmicky, but then gimmicks can be both fun and helpful so give it a try—especially if you find it difficult to develop believable characters.

Make each of your major characters fill out a job application. No, not in the novel. When you start work developing your characters, why not take an application blank (they're available in most office supply stores) or see the forms at the end of this book and fill it out as if you were the character.

If your character is a high-class, high-powered executive, create a resumé. The form you complete will be the basis for the character bio you use as a reference throughout the writing of the book.

Tip #31. Your Characters' Off page/off stage lives.

If you're having a difficult time creating lifelike characters, you probably don't know enough about your people. One way to remedy this is to do an hour-by-hour chronicle of your character's life for a week. It may also be helpful to think in terms of a typical day. For example, what time does your character get up? How does he feel about getting up every morning? Does he bound out of bed with enthusiasm or sort of slither out? Does she drink Red Bull for breakfast or coffee or tea? Who does she call? What time does your character eat breakfast? What does he eat? What does he do next? How does he spend his down time? When and where does he do his laundry? Does he go bowling on Wednesday night? Play poker with the guys on Fridays? Does she get her hair done every Saturday? Have lunch with the same women every Thursday?

All of those things, if you develop a daily calendar, will help you to understand your characters when you are in the early stages of creating them. Doing this schedule will help you another way. Each time a character enters a scene, he or she must come from somewhere. And there will be some carry-over of thought. If you know where your character has been and what's on his or her mind, you'll do a better job of presenting that character as believable.

Remember: People enjoy reading about other people. That's why characterization is so important.

Tip #32. Even Adolph Hitler liked animals.

Adolph Hitler, a heinously deranged villain, liked dogs and was good to his mother. Villains who are all bad just aren't believable because every single human being has some redeeming qualities. You may have to search but they're there. Turnabout's fair play. A totally virtuous character is not believable either. Or interesting. Just as you must get to know your villain's good points, you must get to know your hero's bad ones. What were some of the really nice things your villain once did? What are some of his secret hankerings? What were some of the rotten things your hero did? Okay, maybe not rotten, but embarrassing, stupid or thoughtless?

It's the balance between good and evil and the internal struggle between the two that makes both people and characters interesting.

Tip #33. Change is the essence of life—especially for fictional characters.

As a general rule, your main characters must have changed by the time you write our two favorite words: The End. The change does not always have to be drastic, especially in genre fiction. It can be as simple as your character having learned a lesson, having gained new insight into some formerly perplexing situation, having grown stronger and more self-reliant as a result of the conflicts that make up your plot. Or, depending on your story, your major character may have changed tremendously.

Why is change important? Because change is part of life and if we, as novelists, wish to create believable fiction, we must incorporate change into our characters' lives. Change is also important because without it we have no drama, no conflict, no story.

And how could a reader respect a character who confronts desperate situations and never thinks about the ramifications, never changes, never grows? Smart people learn from their mistakes. So do smart characters. Of course, drama also arises when a character stubbornly refuses to change, but this should not be overdone.

Keep in mind, too, that all change in fiction—as in life—is not for the better. People deteriorate morally, physically, spiritually as well as growing stronger and better. Characters can do the same. Be aware, however, that in most commercial, mass market fiction, the protagonist ultimately must change for the better. The reader of mass market fiction is reading for escape and wants a happy ending or at least a modicum of hope. That's not necessarily the case with literary fiction.

It should also be mentioned that the degree of change does not have to be as extreme in plot-driven novels in genres such as men's adventure, some erotica, and some horror/sci fi/fantasy where the emphasis is on action or plot as opposed to character.

Tip #34. Why not create a family of characters?

As you've already discovered, writing is hard work. Writing well is even harder. Some very successful writers of both commercial and literary fiction have made it easier for themselves by creating a town and/or a set of characters they've used for more than one book.

Think about it. Why can't you create a family of interesting characters? Andrea is the protagonist in this book, her husband Sean or daughter Jennifer could be the protagonist of the next. Or maybe the waitress in the coffee shop, a minor character in this book, is the star of your next production.

Once you create a town or a neighborhood, especially if it's a town or neighborhood you enjoy writing about, a town with interesting attractions and characteristics, you save yourself work. Stephen King's Castle Rock, Maine comes immediately to mind. Or perhaps you're fascinated by an historic era or age.

As the author, you have even more believable settings and characters as a result of both the repetition and the fact that you become more familiar with both. Plus, this gives readers something to collect. This technique worked for William Faulker, Sue Grafton, John Steinbeck and Stephen King to name but a few—why not you?

Use the forms in the workbook section of this book to create and get to know your characters. You'll find they're very interesting people.

Do you really need to know this much about your characters?

YOU BET!

Why?

Because in order to write about a character and bring him or her to life for your reader, you must know that character intimately. One of the main reasons novels are rejected is that the characters are not believable.

Remember: Your character does not merely exist today. He had a life prior to the time your book starts. And you need to know about that life. We are all an accumulation of our lifetime of experiences and those experiences have influenced our personalities, tastes, interests and goals. That works for fictional characters, too.

Remember, two: Characters don't exist only physically in your books. They have thoughts, memories and opinions and you need to know about those thoughts, memories and opinions. In fact, memories are one of the most effective, efficient tools you have as a writer in developing and revealing character.

Psst! When you start complaining because you don't have enough room in the forms provided at the end of this book, you're making real progress.

PENCIL SHARPENER #1: Take one of your favorite books by a favorite author. Re-read the book carefully and write a character sketch of each of the main characters. As you read, make notes of all the different pieces of information the author gave you.

PENCIL SHARPENER #2: Select a person in your life and make a detailed study of that person. Do a biography using these fill-in the blanks as if you were using him as a character. (But don't tell the person what you're doing or she'll want to read and edit what you're writing.)

NOTES:_____

_____

_____

_____

_____

_____

_____

_____

_____

_____

_____

_____

_____

_____

_____

_____

CHAPTER 4: POINT OF VIEW IS MUCH MORE THAN AN EXPRESSION OF OPINION

At this point in your planning, you should have decided on a protagonist, a villain and the genre of the book. Now you should decide on a point of view. That's vital because the point of view you choose is going to affect the plot and the readability of your book. For example, if you decide to do a coming-of-age novel in which your protagonist is a 30-year-old woman and you are going to do it from first person, you cannot interject into this story any other character's thoughts or innermost reactions or reflections. You are locked into the mind and the psyche of your protagonist. (And you'd better have an excellent understanding of a 30-year-old woman's psyche.)

First-person POV does not work too well in action novels because a lot of the suspense is derived from the fact that the reader knows things that your main character doesn't. For example, if you have a main character or a hero who is in a hotel and there's a bomb threat, and the hero doesn't know it, the reader will agonize for him, cheer for him and become emotionally involved. If it's written from the hero's first person POV, the reader knows only what the hero knows and the writer loses the ability to create the same suspense. So the selection of a point of view and the point of view character is an important decision to be made at this point in the planning of your novel.

Omniscient point of view is another form. In this, the story is told from the omniscient author's point of view. The author/god knows and sees and tells all. Ernest Hemingway's work is an excellent example of this. As a writer, you lose emotional contact with your reader, but Hemingway did it skillfully because it matched his world-weary, detached voice.

If you think you want to write from the omniscient point of view, read some Hemingway, observe how he does it, then write a couple of scenes. See if it works for you.

Speaking of point of view, which of course we were, one of the most interesting books written several years ago is Alice Sebold's *The Lovely Bones* and it's especially interesting because of Ms. Sebold's creative choice of a point of view character. Fourteen-year-old Susie Salmon is raped and murdered by a neighbor. She is the viewpoint character, telling her story from heaven. Be forewarned: While trying for originality, realize that fads occur in the publishing world as much as in the arena of high fashion. Quality, that is well-written prose, never goes out of style.

Most importantly, you need to know that you have a choice. Your viewpoint character tells the story; your viewpoint character is the mind, heart, eyes, and ears through which your reader experiences the story. When you are trying to understand what a viewpoint character is, think of it like this: If John is the viewpoint character in a scene, not only is the story told through John's eyes, the reader is privy to everything John sees, hears, smells, tastes, assumes, thinks—the knowledge he has.

Tip #35. How do you select a POV character? Audition him or her.

The decision as to who will be your viewpoint character or characters is one of the most important you will make as you plan your book. And it's important for a number of reasons. If you decide to use a number of viewpoint characters (multiple viewpoint characters), you will probably use one character more than the others. This will probably be your hero or heroine and that's fine.

This one major point-of-view character must be interesting and, as a general rule in category or genre fiction, must be someone the reader likes or at least can relate to throughout the duration of the novel.

As the god/author, you have several choices. You can use first person I as the narrator. There are limitations and advantages to I which we'll discuss in more detail later. You can use second person or you which is even more difficult because you, the writer, will have to keep up that form of reader address for 300-plus pages. Then, there is that workhorse of viewpoint, the third person using she or he. Another option is to use a narrator to regale the reader with the exploits of the hero or heroine a la Dr. Watson. (See Tip #37). But you have to be careful to avoid telling rather than showing.

How do you decide which to use? Choose the viewpoint that feels most comfortable to you and seems the most effective way to tell your story. And remember, too, that your story can be changed. It's not engraved in marble. So, if you start your book in first person and you find that limiting, all you have to do is shift the I to he or she. Write that opening scene or chapter from John's POV using first person I. If it doesn't work, rewrite it from third person, he. In other words, make characters audition for that all important role of POV character.

Tip #36. First person shouldn't necessarily be first choice.

First novels are often written in first person because literary lore has it that most first novels are often thinly disguised autobiographies. Even if that's the case, you don't have to write in first person and you might not want to because there are a number of drawbacks to using first person.

If you're writing from the viewpoint of I, for example, it's very difficult to describe your protagonist. No bathroom or rear view mirrors, please. And you don't want your heroine gazing into a clear lake and describing her features. Reflective surfaces have been used so many times they are truly literary clichés. Furthermore, they are clumsy, boring and predictable.

There are other problems. If you're using I as the viewpoint character, you must be very careful that I does not come off sounding pompous and arrogant. If another character tells the reader that the protagonist is brave, strong-hearted and true, it's more acceptable. If I does it, I sounds self-satisfied and pompous. To counter this, I must confess to some character quirks and flaws and, in this instance, I can end up sounding either weak or neurotic which is okay as long as I is basically likeable from the reader's point of view.

Perhaps the most significant drawback to using I is that, as we discussed above, it limits you, the writer, in creating suspense. One of the most valuable techniques for creating suspense is to place the protagonist in jeopardy. The reader knows that the hero's brakes have been tampered with or that the heroine's wine has been laced with a sleeping draught, but the protagonist doesn't. If I is your point of view character, if you are always in the mind of the hero or heroine as the viewpoint character, there is no way that character and thus your reader can know of the impending danger.

Tip #37. Maybe your hero's best friend should be a blabbermouth.

When you're planning your book, take a good look at the characters. Do you have one who would make a good story teller? This is an especially good choice when your hero performs heroic deeds. Remember how skillfully Arthur Conan Doyle used Dr. Watson to relate Sherlock Holmes' exploits? The stories wouldn't have been nearly as interesting because Holmes would have come across as an insufferable boor if he had spun his own yarns. Dr. Watson was useful in another sense. Doyle used him as a counterpoint. Dr. Watson represents normalcy and points up Holmes' quirks and idiosyncrasies. Keep in mind that your narrator should be a fully developed character, at least in your mind, and should also be interesting in his or her own right.

Tip #38. You don't have to be schizophrenic to write from multiple points of view.

Writing from different point of view characters has any number of advantages. First, it is an excellent tool for developing character. When you are using Mary as a viewpoint character, you are inside Mary's mind and there's no more effective way to reveal her character because you can use her thoughts to show how and what Mary thinks about different situations. You can also use Mary's mind and memories to reveal her past. Let her remember incidents from her childhood or traumatic events. Mary may also think things she would never speak aloud to any other character. The same applies to the next scene when you are in John's mind.

From a purely technical standpoint, switching point of view characters in different scenes (not within a scene—see Tip #40) is an efficient way to keep the plot moving forward. You write one scene using Mary as the viewpoint character in which Mary is getting into the family station wagon to drive home. The next scene may be written from her husband's point of view. He's at home waiting for her, knowing he's tampered with the brakes. The next scene may be written from her daughter's point of view as the child waits for her mother at school, wondering why her mother's late picking her up.

Tip #39. Remember: Each viewpoint character has a different point of view.

Remember that when you're in Mary's mind and body, if she's five foot four inches tall, she's going to have to stretch to reach the top of the bookshelf. John, her husband who's six foot four, can see the dust on the top of the door. Remember too, that John may have a weak ankle from a skiing accident which means that he runs cautiously. Blue is John's favorite color which may mean that when Mary wears a chartreuse dress, John reacts negatively. Or maybe he's color blind which means that Mary must color coordinate his socks and ties. When you are in John's head, the thoughts and memories will be different. They will reflect John's past life.

If Mary's a very traditional Catholic and she sees a nun wearing contemporary dress, she will react, if not verbally, at least mentally. Each character will bring a different frame of reference to his or her perception of the scene. If Mary had a frightening experience with a cat, if she was once lavishly praised for the beauty of her speaking voice, if she failed geometry—these experiences color her outlook on life and affect her attitudes as a point-of-view character.

How do you deal with this? It's really not as hard as it might seem. When you sit down to write a scene, look at your notes. Orient yourself as to where the scene takes place, when, what happens and the identity of your viewpoint character. In the beginning, you may even have to re-read your character's job application. Now take a deep breath and relax. Become Mary or John. Pretend you are your viewpoint character and live the scene as that person. The better you are at doing this, the more your scenes will come to life. And the further along you get in your novel, the easier this will become.

Still doesn't work? Then speak to your characters. Ask them questions. How are you doing, Mary? Are you nervous? Is the car behaving strangely? How are you feeling, John? Nervous, knowing what you've done? Elated? How did it feel to tamper with those brakes?

Blank your mind, relax and wait. This is one of the most intriguing facets of the creative process. If you relax and wait, you'll get your answers. You'll know how your viewpoint character acts and reacts in the scene.

Tip #40. Shiftily shifting viewpoint characters.

It's best not to shift viewpoint characters within a scene. Some writers may argue this point, but it can be very confusing to the reader if you jump into and out of your characters' minds too often and too quickly. For instance, the scene opens and we're in Mary's mind. She's driving along worrying about what to have for dinner. Then suddenly we're in John's mind and he's thinking about the brakes. Then we're back in Mary's mind—all within the same scene. That can be distracting and irritating. It's not skillful writing. Better to plan your scenes so that you have one viewpoint character.

Having said that, there are a couple of instances when you can shift within a scene. For example, if your viewpoint character dies, goes to sleep or loses consciousness, you must (unless you're writing a fantasy) shift into the mind of the conscious character. If you do this, be sure you are in your first viewpoint character's mind long enough so that the reader is comfortable. In other words, don't shift too quickly. Author Charles Todd does this very skillfully in *A Test of Wills*.

PENCIL SHARPENER #1: Here's the set up for the scene. It's a rainy afternoon. John is a school bus driver, Mary is a school teacher riding with her class on a field trip. John and Mary argue about his driving. Write this scene first from John's point of view. See the streets and roads through the windshield as John does. Hear what John hears behind him as he drives. Stay in John's head as he reacts intellectually, physically, and emotionally to Mary's complaints and observations. Now switch! Write the same scene from Mary's point of view. Remember she's sitting somewhere else so she sees everything from a different angle. She is a teacher so she has an entirely different approach and may even try to discipline John as she would one of the children.

PENCIL SHARPENER #2: Select a recent best seller you have enjoyed reading, re-read it to figure out precisely what viewpoint that author chose and then write a paragraph or two explaining why you think the author chose that viewpoint. Go one step further. Critique that writer. Do you think his or her choice of viewpoint character was the most effective choice? Could the writer have derived more emotional content by selecting another character to tell the story in that scene? Look at the book as a whole. Was it written utilizing multiple point-of-view characters? Why? Did it work? Written from first person? Why? Did it work?

NOTES (OR WRITE YOUR SCENE HERE): _____

_____

_____

_____

_____

_____

_____

_____

_____

_____

_____

_____

_____

_____

_____

_____

_____

_____

_____

_____

_____

_____

_____

_____

_____

_____

_____

_____

_____

CHAPTER 5: PLACES AND SETTINGS
ARE NOT THE SAME AS PLACE SETTINGS

Do you spend a great deal of time working on your plots, developing your characters, and worrying about your endings, yet neglect your settings? If so, you're not alone. Many beginning authors fail to appreciate that a well-drawn setting is an excellent dramatic tool. Think about it and you'll see that a setting can be as important as a character in a story. In some instances, it is a character in the story because it affects the outcome, it affects the plot, it affects the actions and reactions and interactions between your characters.

So while you're in the planning stages, give serious thought to your setting and appreciate the richness setting can bring to your book.

To begin, realize that you have choices:
1.   You can use a real town, city or neighborhood.
2.   You can create a fictional town.
3.   You can create a fictional town, basing it on a real town you know well or are willing to research.
4.   You will need both exterior and interior settings.

Now, consider the town or community in which your novel takes place as a character and develop a biographical sketch for this town.

What should a biographical sketch of a town include?

Of course, it will include the basics. You may never need to include some of the following information in your story, but you should know your area intimately. You must know how large your area is, the population, and the different groups that make up that population. Is it a bedroom community for executives who work in industries nearby? Is it a resort area? Is it a farming community where the farms are run by families? Is it an agricultural community where farms are owned by large conglomerates that utilize migrant workers? Is it a community peopled by the very wealthy? Or is it an adjoining community where the residents are people who work for the very wealthy? In other words, who are the people who live in your town? What are the different industries and businesses that make up its economic base?

This information will tell you a lot about what your town looks like, how it functions, and the jobs and positions your characters hold. Additionally, it will affect your characters' daily lives and the size or sophistication of the area you choose will affect their attitudes. It's easier to use a town, village or county that you know as a model for your fictional community or even as the real community itself. This saves time you would otherwise spend on research. And, in addition, research sources are close at hand.

Bottom Line: Knowing your setting can shorten your writing time thus improving your productivity.

Your next step is to create a history for your community. When was it founded? Who were the people who settled it and what did those first settlers contribute to the complexion, the architecture, the economic base, the development of the area? When, or if, did the city incorporate?

Suppose those early settlers had been farmers or bankers or real estate developers? How would they have impacted the area's development? For example, in many young communities in Florida, the first people who moved in were developers, and certainly that has affected and controlled the way those areas have grown. If you're going to create a fictional town or city, develop a composite community based on reality so that you know what it was from its beginning.

And while you're thinking and creating your town, use all five senses because this will enrich your work. If you do this, when you sit down to write a scene, your town will have sounds, smells, rhythms, textures. For example, walking down a sidewalk in an older town, you can feel the texture and the unevenness of the brick under your feet. However, you have much more than merely sounds and sights to work with, so use the other senses. These elements help you build a rich, believable setting, plus they offer you a variety of settings to choose from.

Pretend you're a tourist.

If you are working with a familiar setting, look at the community as if you were a visitor. That's important because when you live in an area, you become desensitized. You no longer see the interesting and new or unusual aspects of your town.

And, don't forget that weather plays an important part in your setting, too. Remember Snoopy, the beagle in the Peanuts comic strip? When he starts a book, he writes, "It was a dark and stormy night." Although that's a cartoon, there's a kernel of truth there because for years we have traditionally expected evil things to happen on dark and stormy nights.

Think about the weather in your community. Does the town suffer through harsh winters? What are the seasonal highs and lows? What are the natural threats to your area? Snowstorms? Hurricanes? Tornadoes? Sandstorms? Does the weather affect the economy? Farming communities, tourist attractions, for example.

Think about sunshine for a moment. If you study vampire lore, you'll know that vampires can go out in the sun after they've reached a certain age of maturity. (You didn't know that? Shame! Your education has been neglected!) I had a lot of fun writing a scene in *Blood Legacy* in which a vampire went on a picnic. It was interesting to write because the ultimate evil was played against a bright sunshiny Florida meadow.

Another example: Think of a child's nursery with its rosy lighting, maybe a clown lamp on the nightstand, and the cradle rocking gently. You'd never think of anything evil happening there. That's an effective place to plant evil because readers are not expecting it and because finding evil there engages their emotions. One of the most gripping scenes I've ever read was about a snake in a child's nursery, crawling along through air conditioning ducts in the ceiling. Scared me silly.

And consider the reverse: a maximum security prison where one inmate befriends and helps another. The excitement of the unpredictable!

Contrast heightens emotional impact.

For example, if you want to write a novel about a troubled marriage, you might use one of the resorts in the Pocono Mountains where the rooms have the heart-shaped beds and bathtubs, where everything is pink. Wouldn't that be a great setting for a couple struggling to save or end a marriage? In this case, you are playing against your setting, which can be a very effective tool, as well as using your setting to heighten the effect. In a sense it's like black and white. They play off one another so well because the white makes the black look blacker, and the black makes the white look whiter. They intensify one another.

And as with every other aspect of writing, specific detail is essential in creating scenes. Don't write, "There was a gorgeous tree." Gorgeous is in the mind of the beholder. Show the tree's beauty. Describe it. Paint a word picture of the sunbeams glinting off the tender, green leaves. The reader wants to know what kind of tree it is, whether its trunk is straight or gnarled and whether it has small leaves, and whether it is sick or dying. And how much more interesting to read about a queen palm, an Areca palm or a scrub oak than a tree?

Small details deftly woven into your description and dialogue lend credibility and color to your settings and your entire book. They also provide one of the few places where using adjectives adds to your writing.

But you must be accurate. If, for example, you write a story about Alaska in which you mention a date palm, your reader will be jarred and you will lose his cooperation, his willing suspension of disbelief.

Outdated travel books are a good source of information about an area, and they are cheaper than the new ones. Buy them when they are two or three years old. Buy them at garage and book sales. Unless you're an avid gardener and know a great deal about botany, collect books on plants and trees. Even seashells, if your area is near a beach or shore. That way when you mention a specific plant, you can be sure that plant grows where you put it.

You might also collect language books at garage and book sales. You never know when you're going to need the foreign phrase for, "Stop that vampire!" Or, perhaps you are doing a scene in a foreign country and need the language for a road sign. If you can use the foreign words, your work is more colorful and credible. And now, of course, we have the internet!

The writer as interior designer.

When you sit down to work on your sets, let me share and at the same time attribute a tip. I was very fortunate to have Mona Kent Eddy as a friend. Mona was a very successful radio writer in the 1930s through the 1950s. She wrote popular radio serials titled "Portia Faces Life" and "Captain Midnight" as well as a TV soap called "Woman With A Past."

Mona explained that when you sit down to create and write a scene, you should envision drawing down a blank, white movie screen. Then dress that screen as you would a stage. Put in your carpet and know what your carpet looks like. Put in ceiling fixtures and furniture. Place windows and bookshelves and select the objects of art and different accessories that will be of use in the room.

Incidentally, this is an especially helpful technique if you are having a problem with the old bugaboo of "showing instead of telling." If you can envision in your mind the action of your scene as taking place in front of you on that white screen, you will notice that your heroine has a habit of blushing when she hears the hero's name, or that the hero has a habit of scratching his nose when he's nervous. You'll see them, they become real to you, and it will be easier for you to show the reader what you're seeing.

Introduce your readers to the set.

As with characters, the first time you introduce your readers to a new setting, you must give them enough detail so that they can recreate in their minds the scene that you have created in yours and communicated via the written word. Think of your readers as being in a theater. As the curtain rises, the playgoer registers the appearance of the set. You're creating a theater, too, a theater of the mind.

Actually, developing settings parallels the process of developing characters—and both parallel real life. When you first meet a person, you notice height, weight, age, generalities. As you get to know that person better, you observe the smaller details, the more intimate aspects of the person's life and personality. It's the same with settings. Think of that when introducing a new setting for the first time and present it as if it were a new person.

As you get into the scene and the book, sprinkle in the details. A sentence or phrase of description spread through several paragraphs of dialogue or action will not slow the action.

You don't want to begin a chapter with six or seven long paragraphs of description, but it is important that you set the stage for your reader.

Since you are creating a theater of the mind, when you first introduce a setting, you must also think in terms of your point of view character. Through whose eyes is the reader seeing the setting? For example, if a child as your POV character walks into the room, depending on the age of course, a child would have to look up. And would see a large room filled with tall people. A child's perception because of height and experience is naturally different from that of an adult entering this room.

Another example: A mother who walks into her son's bedroom is going to notice the mess first. That's the mother's point of view. The boy's girlfriend might come in and notice the posters of the rock stars on the wall or her photo on his dresser.

When you introduce a setting through a specific character's eyes, you must remember to see it yourself through that character's eyes.

Sometimes at the beginning of a chapter when you are setting the scene with the expository material that readers need, you may write from the omniscient point of view. But, as always, follow the logic.

When we enter a room, we first notice the size in proportion to ourselves, how comfortable we are, how big the room is. Then, we notice the color scheme. And it's after we have recorded those general impressions, that we begin to observe the wrinkled linen tablecloth, the threadbare carpet and the specific individual details of the room.

So, when you introduce a setting, the first thing you and your reader want to observe is the size. Next is the color scheme and then the details such as the artwork, the furniture, and the condition of the room. Neat? Messy? Shabby? New?

Red alert: If there's a bloody body in that room the viewer, the reader, is not going to notice the Dhurri rug. Describe the body first. This sounds simple, but it's amazing how many times beginning writers make this mistake.

Also keep in mind that when you have created a highly emotionally charged scene in which the interaction between the characters is more important than the setting, try not to play that scene against a setting with a great deal of natural activity. For example, if you have a man with a very bad heart condition and he's arguing with a woman and the reader is afraid the man is going to have a heart attack and die, don't place that man in a hurricane shelter without giving it a lot of thought.

Why? Because the scene will be loaded with sensory information such as the sound of the winds outside, the thud of the rain against the walls, the emotions of the people in the hurricane shelter, the other conversations. You must include these if you are going to recreate that scene vividly. However, if you do, you have the two dramas competing with one another.

If you want to do something like that and you want to heighten the suspense and surprise, don't give him the heart attack in the middle of the hurricane, let him get through the hurricane safely, go home to his house which is safe and sound, and drop dead on the doorstep.

Perhaps you want to write a book with scenes in foreign places that you haven't visited. It's not impossible, but you must do your research. You must check and doublecheck every fact in your description. In this instance, landmarks can be a useful tool. For example, if you are setting a scene in Paris, go on line to research the Eiffel Tower, the Arc de Triomphe or Notre Dame Cathedral. That's a good example of literary shorthand because when readers read the name, they immediately conjure a mental image of Paris. You now have two things going for you. First, you have established the area, and second, you have gotten the reader to do some of your work for you.

But once you have established the area by means of the Eiffel Tower, the Empire State Building, the Lincoln Memorial, once you've done that at the beginning of the scene, you must sprinkle in street names or the names of shops that you can find by going online or something that further delineates the area. If you do this, you have, for most purposes, established this scene credibly in your reader's mind.

For more information, go to your travel agency and get the travel brochures. The staff will give you names of places to write for more background information. And you can write to the embassies or tourism bureaus. Many of these countries have tourism bureaus here in this country and their function is to provide information.

Realize, too, that the type of book will affect your setting. For example, if you're writing a detective or crime novel, you might describe a ghetto in your chosen city where the plate glass storefront windows have been broken and repaired with tape, an abandoned car, a tire iron lying on the pavement or men loitering in the shadows. If you are writing a romance, you might use the same town, but include different details. For instance, you might describe a movie theatre marquee and the movie playing will be a well-known romance. The air will be rife with the scent of flowers. You may have a handsome, virile man striding down the street. In other words, the objects you choose to include your descriptions will and must depend on the type of book and scene you're writing. You can also play against type as in the nursery with the snake.

The next important point is that description is not just a list. If you were to describe the room in which you're sitting as you read this book, you might say that it's a room with a coffee and two end tables, that it has seating for eight and that it's twelve feet long by eighteen feet wide. That's an inventory.

If you choose to describe the room from the viewpoint of a political candidate who's seeking a donation to his campaign, the first thing he spots is the couple who own the home sitting together on the sofa. He'll notice the quality of the furnishings, the way the home is kept. From these details, he'll deduce whether they can afford to make a donation and how much it will be. But he'll begin with size, color scheme and then details. And every detail included should be there for a purpose. They should not be there by accident. That's sloppy writing.

Remember that you may be forced to use mundane settings such as a den to reinforce your characters. Let's take a character who is a lawyer, a workaholic, and whose main interest is the law. Chances are that his bookshelves are loaded with law books, political biographies, and books about government. You probably will not find books on gardening or travel. The biographies he reads will show the reader a lot about his political persuasion.

Or say you have a small study in a home with teenagers and your characters are struggling to make ends meet. They won't have a huge desk of hand-carved mahogany. They may have a desk that they picked up at Goodwill for ten or fifteen dollars. It may have some initials carved in the top of it, maybe one leg is uneven, maybe the castor is missing and they have a matchbook under one leg, unless the husband is handy, which is another story. You are the creator so make all of these details work for your book. Don't just say desk. Make it a specific color of desk, a condition of desk. Let it tell us something about the characters.

Using brand names.

As writers we are constantly battling to earn the reader's suspension of disbelief. Let's say you have a scene in which a vampire walks into a room. If the setting is as bizarre as the idea of a vampire, the reader will have difficulty believing the book, but if that vampire walks past a TV on which a rerun of "Family Ties" is playing and he sits at the dinner table and there's Blue Willow china in front of him, if there's a bottle Chianti on the sidebar or the buffet, you've got him interacting with reality and the reader will decide your world is real. The reader will give you that, for the period of this book—X number of pages—vampires do exist.

Brand names can be a very effective tool. A can of soup brings one image to your mind. A can of Campbell's tomato soup gives you a very vivid picture. Maybe a can of Progresso minestrone brings a different picture to your mind. Common sense will keep you from writing negatively about a named product. You don't want to be sued.

Let characters interact with the setting and the physical props.

Remember that your characters must react to their surroundings. They must react emotionally, physically and cerebrally. In other words, they must react with their minds and their recollections, their feelings and their opinions. Perhaps they walk into a room and they think, Wow! What a carpet. Or, Gee, I hate those chartreuse drapes. Let them think that because that's normal. Don't let them go on about it, but it is normal for a human being and, therefore, for a character to react to settings.

If a character walks into a room, the character should not merely interact with the furniture, i.e., sitting down, leaning against, etc., but should also be aware of the sounds in the room, the smells, the texture of the chair he or she sits in.

This is important: To create well-written, believable settings, you must sharpen your powers of observation. You can jolt your senses, by putting yourself in unfamiliar situations. When you go about the business of your everyday life, vary your routes. If, for example, you go to the same place to work every day or the same grocery store, give yourself a thrill and take different routes. It's good not to know where things are. To have to ask, to have to look, to be in an unfamiliar situation.

Our world has become disturbingly uniform. In nearly every city, you'll find Kentucky Fried Chicken, McDonald's, and Burger King and Shell and Mobil gas stations instead of the old family businesses. Stay alert and see the differences. They're still there.

If you do this, you'll have taken an important step toward avoiding clichés in your settings. But you must also be thoughtful. For example, if you are working on a book with the theme of how corrupting corporate power is or the tragedy of a doomed romance, a big city may be the first setting you think to use. But how much more powerful is it to have a romance go wrong in a small town where everyone knows everyone else or when it's a one company town and everyone is affected? You have the power of choice; use it.

In other words, avoid clichés in your settings. Think in terms of the place where you can best and most effectively tell your story. And, if you elect to write about the place you know best, don't be concerned about being labelled a regional author. John D. MacDonald didn't worry about being considered regional. William Faulker wasn't concerned. Nor was Eudora Welty. Write about the places you know, you love, or the places you enjoy writing about.

Bottom Line: Set your book in the place where you can best tell your story.

Tip #41. Get 'em out of the house and the office.

The term armchair traveler has special significance to the contemporary fiction writer. While you should not contrive to position your characters in places that are not germane to the context of the story, look around your fictional landscape. If, for example, your protagonists are quarreling, must they do it at home? Why not let them argue in a zoo, a gambling casino, a fudge factory, a Tarot reader's den? An upscale restaurant?

Make it a point to check your outline for dull settings. Writers so often think in terms of living rooms. Or kitchens, bedrooms and offices. While some of these settings can be utilized effectively, don't use them too often. Other settings can be used as a backdrop for the action. The opening of an art exhibit. A skating rink. A shopping mall with soap opera stars who've flown in to make special appearances. A school play or a school pageant. In other words, select interesting, unusual places for as many scenes as you can. Notice how your favorite writers utilize settings. The choice of a setting is not an accident, it's a conscious, deliberate decision.

Remember: Readers read to escape, to learn and to experience new things. If possible, take your readers to places they've never been and may never go.

Tip #42. Setting the stage—interior design tips for novelists.

The most successful interior decorators plan their projects to reflect the tastes of their clients. It follows that fiction writers should create settings that reflect the tastes of their characters. This means that if one of your characters is a child psychologist, he or she might have worn copies of Dr. Seuss's *Cat In The Hat* and/or books by Judy Blume on the bookshelves along with classic psychological texts and reference books. On the wall will be the diplomas. Your psychologist has a personal life as well. This means she will have photos of her husband, children, golf or tennis trophies, perhaps a chessboard with a game in progress.

The places a character lives, works and plays can and should be used by the fiction writer to reveal important information about that character.

Tip #43. Don't dump description in clumps.

Big chunks of description are visually off-putting to readers because their eyes can be overwhelmed by a huge mound of gray type. As a result, they'll skim those passages. Granted, the writer must set the stage when the scene first opens. The reader has the right to know when and where the action is happening. However, clumps of description—unless written skillfully and interspersed with activity on the part of your characters—can slow the pace of the novel. It's much more effective to dole out description a phrase and a dollop at a time. If you can't avoid it, break your text into shorter paragraphs.

Tip #44. Whether weather—sure it can be a cliché, so use it creatively.

For years, every novel opened with a description of the weather. Makes sense. As human beings, weather has a tremendous impact on us both consciously and unconsciously. It's such a vital part of life (and fiction) we can't eliminate it entirely. Additionally, it serves a very real function. The wise writer uses weather to create plot complications, establish settings and define the mood. The wise writer, however, tries to avoid the obvious. A dark, rainy night doesn't always have to presage disaster. A sunny day does not infallibly spell delightful doings.

Weather, skillfully used, can be a potently effective tool, a backdrop, almost another character. It can be used as a contrast to heighten the mood, create irony or a sense of suspense. The trick in writing about the weather is to be as unpredictable as the weather itself.

Tip #45. What's real, what isn't? Using fictional locations in real towns.

Certainly, you can create fictional locations in real towns and cities. It's done all the time. Sometimes—especially if the story takes place in the town where you live—it's more comfortable to do so. The use of real places lends a note of authenticity to your writing. Especially if you know or research the area very thoroughly so that you can accurately and precisely re-create the ambience as well as describing it physically. Just make sure your fictional businesses are located in actual business sections and homes in residential communities and remember to include variety.

If the setting is a privately-owned actual business, you're safer not using it if something takes place in your book that could have a negative impact on the business. If what you write could affect the business, you're better off either creating a totally fictional setting or thoroughly disguising it and even having a lawyer check the final manuscript. Don't leave it up to the publishers—contracts today no longer protect the writer at the publisher's expense.

Tip #46. Your chance to be a big-time developer.

If you've decided to create the town, city or subdivision in which your novel takes place, get organized. Begin by preparing your own map. Define the basic area by sketching a rough outline. On what street does your hero live? Put it on the map. Where does he work? Where is the elementary school? Drugstore? Doctor's office? Police station? Each time you use a new location, new building, you should name and place it on your map.

This method will help you avoid inconsistencies—First National Bank won't front on Oak Street in one scene and on Banker's Boulevard in the next. It will also help you to move your characters physically from one location to another. It can also help you create a more believable, realistic, interesting setting.

Tip #47. Being a writer means vacations will never be the same.

From now on, your vacations will do double duty—first, as a reviving break from your regular routine, and, second, as an opportunity to scout locations for scenes and books. This means you'll view and measure every town, city, police station, courthouse, restaurant, tourist attraction or historical site as a possible setting. Is it different? Unique? Interesting? Beautiful? Ugly? Does it have a history? Could you use it for a scene? What kind of scene—happy, sad, ominous?

If you go someplace and you see a setting that might be of use to you later, take pictures of it. Photograph interesting restaurants, stores, pretty streets, beautiful old homes, courthouses, morgues, the outside of the morgue, whatever. Take several pictures from different viewpoints. When you are looking for a setting in the real world, go around to the back of the building as well. And look at it from both sides. When you get home, file them under different categories of settings—homes, office buildings, restaurants.

Get a map. Buy postcards. Visit bookstores to pick up regional histories not available in other areas. Take home local newspapers and magazines. Visit the chamber of commerce and load up on brochures and business cards. Write down the name and address of the chamber of commerce and the state tourism bureau. Once you're home should you have a question, you have a source of information.

Take a supply of 9 x 12 or 10 x 13 manila envelopes and slap your address labels on them. Take postage so you can mail materials home. That way you won't have to tote them around.

Remember: Just as with characters, you will always need to know more about your setting than your reader. In other words, you will never use every piece of information you generate by filling out the Checklist for Settings or Interior Checklist in the worksheets section of this book. The importance of this exercise is that it will enable you to know your setting better and thus you will write more knowledgably and credibly about it.

PENCIL SHARPENER #1: Go to your local supermarket. How big is it? How wide are the aisles? How are the products organized? What are the colors? Really look at the shoppers, notice what they are buying. Notice the little scars on the cheek, or the patterns of baldness. Notice all of these things because this exercise will help you develop an observant eye so essential to writing vivid, effective description. Make notes. Think of what could happen in the supermarket. Once you're home, write a scene that takes place in the supermarket.

PENCIL SHARPENER No. #2: Go to the emergency room of a local hospital and just sit there. (Don't let them treat you regardless of what they say.) Sit there and really watch and listen. Jot down conversations. What are the sounds? What are the expressions on the faces? What is the body language telling you? What are the smells? What do the footsteps sound like when they are coming down that long hall? What does the wheelchair sound like as nurses or orderlies wheel it down that long hall? How do people react to stress?

PENCIL SHARPENER #3: Go to an airport, a bus station or a railroad terminal. What does the terminal look like? Again, observe. Make notes. What do the travelers look like? Ages? Dress? Attitudes? How do they part, if leaving. How do they greet each other when people arrive? Watch and write a scene utilizing your notes and the human drama you observe.

NOTES:_____

_____

_____

_____

_____

_____

_____

_____

_____

_____

_____

_____

_____

_____

_____

_____

_____

_____

_____

_____

_____

_____

_____

CHAPTER 6: DIALOGUE IS MORE
THAN PEOPLE TALKING

So often beginning writers dread and avoid writing dialogue. The man reason is usually that they aren't comfortable with punctuating dialogue. A few simple rules solve that problem:

1. Start a new paragraph every time a different character speaks.
2. Put quotation marks at the beginning of the character's speech. Put quotation marks at the end.
3. Where do you put the punctuation marks? Let's say you write this dialogue: Mary said, "I'll be home by dinnertime." Notice the placement of the comma and the period. It's that simple.
4. If your character speaks a long passage, you may want to break it up into two or more paragraphs. If you do, put quotation marks at the beginning of each paragraph, but do not put closing quotation marks at the end of each paragraph, only at the end of the speech, the last paragraph of the speech. For example (Bear in mind that this is not necessarily an example of good writing, just punctuation.):

"We'll meet you at the malt shop," Mary yelled to Cassandra as she and Elizabeth crossed the parking lot at Altamont High School. "I don't know what Cassandra sees in George. He's ugly, not too bright, and sometimes I think he's deliberately rude. I can't help but wonder if she goes out with him just to make her father mad. But what a price to pay. Can you imagine doing anything that stupid? I mean spending your free time with somebody you don't like just to tick off your parents? I mean like that's so not cool.

"What do you want to bet he shows up at the malt shop?" Mary continued as she and Elizabeth climbed into Elizabeth's fire engine red Mustang convertible.

When writing dialogue, you must keep in mind your character's level of education, type of work (is there jargon typical of that position), and the area of the country where the character was born and raised.

Tip #48. Dialogue is more than straight talk.

Dialogue serves a number of purposes. It imparts information, moves the plot forward, reveals character and emotion.

And dialogue not only can, but must do all of these.

Economy in dialogue is the hallmark of the skilled, professional writer. That passage of dialogue between John and Mary we discussed earlier in which she returns home safely after having had the brakes fail must serve all of these purposes. It must reveal John's reaction, Mary's reaction and indicate what John is going to do next.

Tip #49. What was he doing when he said that?

One of the most common mistakes beginning writers make when writing dialogue is in recording only the spoken and omitting the unspoken dialogue. A man who is nervous does not merely stutter. He lowers his gaze. (He does not drop his eyes nor do they wander out the window, but that's another topic.) He plays with his tie, bites his nails, paces back and forth.

Compare your characters to stage actors. They use the set. They play against the set. If the hero is feeling cocky, he plops himself down at the desk, leans back in the chair and puts his feet up. If there's a coffee maker on the set, he pours himself a cup of coffee.

Your characters should interact with the set as actors do, which is what they are. And you must intersperse the dialogue with physical action and thoughts. However, don't force your character to twiddle his thumbs just to interject physical action. The physical action should be something your character would naturally do.

Something else to keep in mind: The closer you get to the climax of the book, the more you'll want to keep your dialogue honed to heighten the effect of things happening rapidly. But in perhaps the first third of the book, use dialogue as a method of dispersing the description while moving the plot forward.

Tip #50 He said, she said…

Don't worry if you have a lot of he saids and she saids. Variety is nice, but said works—unless the way something is said is as important or more important than what is said. So, if two characters are talking and the content of the dialogue is what counts, said will do fine. On the other hand, if one of the characters says something innocuous, but his or her tone of voice or manner of address is important, use a more colorful verb.

One other thought: If you delineate, both by order of who's speaking and the manner of speaking—accent, pet phrases, educational background relevant to the character—precisely which character is talking, you do not have to attribute every single speech. This is especially appropriate in a two-party conversation. Establish that John is speaking first and Bryan is speaking second. Then you don't need "John said" and "Bryan said" every time.

Tip #51. The voice in your character's mind…internal dialogue.

Sit quietly. Do you hear that voice in your mind? Sometimes that mental dialogue goes nonstop, doesn't it? It's not always positive either (that's another book!). Your viewpoint character in each scene should have an internal voice, too. You can make excellent use of that voice to reveal many things—information about the plot that your character can reveal to the reader but not the other characters, information about the character himself or herself (back story) including his or her opinions, attitudes and emotions.

Tip #52. Seen, but not heard?

Sometimes a character's facial expressions are as revealing as what he or she says or doesn't say. And sometimes the facial expressions and body language diametrically contradict what the character says. Body language and facial expressions can be useful tools in creating both plot complications and suspense.

The television set is the best text you can possibly have when it comes to this technique. Soap operas, in particular. Now don't get hooked—you can't afford to waste the time. But tune in to the different soap opera programs for several days running. Listen, both with the sound on and off and you'll see this fictional technique in action.

Tip #53. Eavesdropping is key to writing successful dialogue.

People and actual conversation are the best sources of information and inspiration for writing successful dialogue. Train yourself to eavesdrop. Discreetly, of course. But wherever people gather, you'll have a source. Supermarkets in the check-out lines. Airports. Bus stations. Emergency rooms at your local hospital. Remember, you cannot use actual dialogue. Not because it's illegal, but because it's too verbose. And boring! The dialogue you write must be much, much more concise than actual speech.

Bottom Line: You are listening to conversations to sensitize yourself to speech patterns, colloquial expressions, tones of voice.

Tip #54. You don't have to tell the reader everything your character hears.

As you continue studying this art/craft, you'll run across a discussion of the unwritten contract that exists between the reader and the writer. As was mentioned earlier, basically, the idea is this: While demanding that your work be believable enough to convince him, the reader will permit you to omit or alter certain commonly known and accepted information.

For example: In the real world:

> Kathy greets Mary by saying, "Hello, Mary. How are you? I haven't seen you in a long time."
> And Mary responds, "Hi, Kathy. I'm just fine. How are you? How are your children? And that nice husband of yours?"
> Kathy continues, "Mary, has Ted recovered from his automobile accident yet?"

In fiction, the reader will permit you to omit most of that passage. If what you're really working toward is getting Mary to discuss Ted's condition, that same passage will read something like this:

"Mary," Kathy asked, concern darkening her blue eyes, "how's Ted doing?"

Mary shook her head. "Not well."

Wordy dialogue is one dead giveaway of a writer's amateur status. If you're not comfortable writing dialogue, keep it short. Get to the point.

And move right on to the next point.

No loitering or filibustering allowed in well written fiction.

Tip #55. How do you indicate thoughts?

It used to be absolutely imperative that thoughts be underlined. That underlining by the way, was a signal to the editor and the typesetter that the underlined passage was to be set in italics. Today many publishers have gotten away from the italics and use body type for thoughts, but the choice is yours. Don't be reluctant to use thought as a verb to make this clear: I wish I was back home with Auntie Em, Dorothy thought wistfully. Thought is as unobtrusive and as useful as said.

You should, however, be very careful in the use of quotation marks. Quotation marks tell the reader the passage has been spoken aloud.

Tip #56. Non sequiturs and other foreign phrases.

While you must not attempt to replicate every word in fictional dialogue that you hear in actual dialogue, you can borrow stylistic pointers from real conversations. For example, while having a conversation with your husband or wife or parent, you may ask something and not only does he fail to answer your question, he changes the subject.

"I wonder how Mrs. Knowles next door is doing," Mary said to Jim.

Seated comfortably in the recliner in front of the television set, Jim clicked the remote control surfing between channels. "Did you hear that the convenience store two blocks over got robbed last night? Thieves got away with a small fortune."

This is an example of a non sequitur, a Latin phrase meaning not in sequence or not following in order. Real conversation is not structured, not organized. Human beings do not completely finish discussing one topic before moving on to the next. Human beings quite often do not express themselves in complete sentences.

And they use contractions, saying don't for do not, won't for will not, and so on. Using do not instead of don't sounds stilted and unnatural unless (take a lesson from actress Bette Davis) your character has something very important to say in which case he or she may speak very deliberately and avoid contractions.

As for foreign phrases, don't use them unless you absolutely must. If you must, be sure they are used in a context that makes them easily understandable.

And foreign phrases that are uncommon must be set in italics.

Tip #57. A dash of accent goes a long way.

When you have a character with a foreign background, you must be extremely careful that his dialogue is easily understood by the reader. There's nothing more irritating to a reader than to be caught up in a well-paced story and then dragged to a halt while he tries to figure out what the character is saying. To avoid this, keep the dialect and accent to a minimum. Just enough to give the reader the flavor of the foreign language. A dash of accent. Where possible, instead of trying to recreate the language by means of spelling, try to listen to people who speak the language and recreate their sentence structures and rhythms.

Tip #58. What can you do if your characters sound alike?

If your characters sound alike, it means you do not know them well enough to write about them. There are several solutions.

First: Read the passages of dialogue aloud. Listen carefully. Do the characters sound like themselves? Does the auto mechanic sound like the CEO. or the grandmotherly nurse? If not, are you using (but not overusing) the language and jargon of that trade or profession? Does the dialogue reflect that character's educational and social background? Are you using the terminology in context so that the average reader can understand or figure it out?

Second: Go back and study your characters again. Get to know them even better. Go back into their childhoods. Create or learn about the turning points in their lives.

Third: Create a schedule for your character. That helps you to get to know your character better. It also helps because when your character enters a scene, you'll know where he was just prior to that entrance. This will help you portray him as a real person with a life even when he's not appearing on stage and he'll have more to talk about. (See workbook page A Week in the Life of _____ on page 188).

Fourth: You might also sit quietly for a moment. Call your character by name and ask—aloud if you wish and if you're alone—what's wrong, where you're going wrong. Wait quietly for a moment or two and you may be surprised when you get your answer.

When really in trouble, remember to keep the dialogue brief, trim it to the bare bones. Then leave only the marrow.

Knowing your character's normal routine will also be of help in plotting. It will help you to know what is unusual in his life and you may derive ideas from what he usually does.

PENCIL SHARPENER #1: Leave a cell phone or tape recorder in the middle of the dinner table. Tape the dinner conversation, then transcribe 10 or 15 minutes of it using the proper punctuation as if you were writing in a scene. Now edit it, but be aware of the non sequiturs, the ignored and unanswered questions, the physical actions of the people sitting at the table as they speak and the repetition. There's bound to be a lot of repetition. When you have edited the actual conversation, rewrite it, interspersing the gestures, facial expressions, and body language.

PENCIL SHARPENER #2: Pick a favorite author, one whose dialogue you admire. Copy two or three pages of the dialogue. It's all right. You're not going to plagiarize it. Now read it aloud. And since it's not yours, edit it to the bare bones. See if you can make it better. Figure out what that author does that you don't.

NOTES:_____

_____

_____

_____

_____

_____

_____

_____

_____

_____

_____

_____

_____

_____

_____

_____

_____

_____

_____

_____

_____

_____

_____

_____

_____

_____

_____

_____

CHAPTER 7: IT'S EASIER SEEN IN A SCENE

As with every aspect of writing, you have choices when it comes to creating scenes. Nearly every scene contains a setting, external and internal dialogue, emotion, conversation and physical action. The proportion will determine the type of scene; i.e., whether it's cerebral, emotional, physical or conversational.

Your job is to determine which type of scene will move your story forward most effectively. The content of some scenes will leave you no choice, but a word of warning may help. If you are writing an extremely emotional scene, keep the language simple, sentences short. Don't go in for dramatic, emotion-ridden words. It will be overkill and melodramatic. The sincerity will be destroyed.

Tip #59. Create the tapestry of your novel by using variety in the placement and emotional color of your scenes.

Think of your novel as a wall hanging, a tapestry that tells a story. The wall hanging is created from thousands, tens of thousands of individual threads of different colors and, sometimes, of different weights and materials. Your tapestry is composed of words, sentences and scenes rather than thread and you must vary the color from the standpoint of content. In structuring your plot, remember that you do not want too many scenes of one color together. You do not, as a rule, want one scene involving a fist fight followed immediately by another containing physical action (unless, of course, you are creating a montage effect of fighting scenes because that is the foundation of your book).

You achieve pace and depth and maintain your reader's interest by using variety. This means you may follow a scene involving action with a quiet, cerebral scene in which your characters are thoughtful or reflective followed by a scene involving some form of love whether it's friendship or ardor. Stringing together a series of scenes with the same emotional content is disturbing, even boring to the readers. They may not know what's wrong, but they will sense that something is.

Tip #60. Each scene has a beginning, middle, and end...an internal structure.

Having said that, as we discussed earlier, you do NOT have to beginning at the beginning or end at the end. For example, let's say John and Mary have a discussion that escalates into a horrendous argument. At the climax of the scene and the argument, Mary slaps John. After that, the scene is resolved as they make up. You, as the author, have five choices or options.

First: You can open the scene with the discussion and follow the sequence of events within the scene sequentially and chronologically.

Second: You can open your scene moments before the slap, have a brief flashback—perhaps in the form of internal dialogue in the mind of your viewpoint character in which the argument is briefly relived—and then move forward to the resolution of scene and argument.

Third: You can begin at the beginning and end the scene when Mary slaps John leaving the reader to wonder what happens next.

Fourth: You can begin your scene right after the slap and then tell the back story of what led to it and move forward through the reconciliation.

Fifth: You can begin your scene while John and Mary are making up, reveal what led to the argument in back story. And not show the argument at all.

Bottom line: You have choices, options. Use them. Enjoy them.

Tip #61. The scene opens. What must you tell your reader up front?

As a general rule, each time you begin a scene you must give your reader some basic information. Your reader is entitled to know the following at once:

1. Where the scene takes place.
2. The identity of the viewpoint character.
3. How much time has elapsed since the previous scene.
4. When the present scene is happening.

If you don't include this information, you will confuse and irritate the reader who may well skim through your precious prose until he reaches this information skipping other important details.

Remember: It bears repeating. You are trying to make real an unreal world. By setting the events of your story against a backdrop of reality—i.e., a specific place, specific time—you heighten the sense of credibility. Think about it. When you enter an unfamiliar place, you immediately orient yourself as to where you are and what time it is. This is the way readers orient themselves at the beginning of each scene.

Tip #62. Being unpredictable contributes to being readable, but...

We've discussed the importance of varying the coloring and content of the scenes in your book. It's important to vary the structure of your scenes as well. However, the story is always the most important element. Your question to yourself must always be: How can I best tell this story so that I will entertain, inform, and enlighten my reader? Content should never be subjugated to form. Form should always serve content.

Tip #63. Practice safe sex, especially on paper.

Sex—unless you are writing erotica or pornography and there is a definite difference—never sells a book in and of itself. You still need a good story and interesting characters. Sex between two fictional characters should not be thrown in to sell a book. It should be there—to whatever degree—because it is a natural outgrowth of the relationship between the two characters.

How explicit should you be? This varies from writer to writer and decade to decade. In general, when making this decision:

First: Figure out who your readers will be and what they expect and will be comfortable with.

Second: Figure out where your own personal boundaries lie and, if you choose to go beyond these, do so.

Keep in mind your book is a concrete item that will be around a long time, if not on the shelves of a bookstore, then in a reader's mind and bookshelf. However far you decide to go in your intimate scenes, remember to include the emotions and thoughts of your characters. You want to avoid using the anatomical laundry list approach to sex which is characterized by a list of body parts and physiological reactions. Same rules for profanity. If it's appropriate to your novel, and you're comfortable using it, fine. Excellent books are written that include or exclude profanity. The choice is yours.

Tip #64. Writing sensibly, sensitively, sensually…

One of the most effective ways to bring to life a lackluster scene is to think about it sensually. In other words, when you edit the scene check to be sure you have included all the senses: Visual—colors and images; smell—the odors and aromas of the different elements in the scene; sound—the noises that occur in your scene above and beyond the characters' voices, sounds so normal they can be easily omitted, but are so natural they add dimension and credibility. Taste—does not have to relate to food, can relate to fear, to a pervasive odor in the atmosphere; texture—the clothes a hero wears will have a weight and a feel, so will the tree trunk he leans against and the mud sucking at his bare feet.

PENCIL SHARPENER #1: Pick any of the books of best-selling authors James Patterson or Sidney Sheldon. They write in scenes. Type a couple of their scenes to get a feel for how important it is to establish time, place, point of view character.

PENCIL SHARPENER #2: Read and dissect at least three sex scenes. Romance novels are excellent sources for these. Nora Roberts writes some humdingers! Highlight in red every body part mentioned. Highlight every emotion in pink. Use yellow for physical action. Use blue for thoughts. Use green for description of the setting. This will give you an excellent breakdown of the structure of any scene, including sex scenes.

PENCIL SHARPENER #3: Mojo John and Conjure Mary are standing in front of the monkey cage at the New Orleans Zoo. They are arguing about John's involvement with Marie Laveau. Write the argument scene from John's point of view. Now write the same scene from Mary's point of view. Begin the second scene from a different point in the scene.

NOTES:_____

_____

_____

_____

CHAPTER 8: GETTING AHEAD IN TIME AND PLACE A/K/A TRANSITION AND EXPOSITION

Transition is an important element of fiction writing because if you don't handle it properly, you confuse your reader. In fact, one of the signs of an inexperienced writer is an abrupt transition.

Writing effective, efficient transitions is not difficult—as long as you keep the reader in mind. Remember that any time you begin a new scene, you must indicate how much time has elapsed since the previous scene, where the scene is taking place, and identify the point of view character. If you do this, you'll go a long way toward avoiding reader confusion.

Mechanically speaking, you can indicate a new scene several ways. Begin by hitting your enter key twice so that you leave four spaces. That white space signals the reader that the one scene has ended and a new one is about to begin.

Some writers prefer to intersperse a line of asterisks. This is perfectly acceptable and it won't really matter how you handle it in the manuscript because the copy editor will make your manuscript consistent to the publishing house's style manual. (The current thinking is that asterisks are jarring to the reader. In other words, they take the reader out of the story because the asterisks are not part of it. Whatever you're feeling about the lowly asterisk, your goal as a writer is always to write a book so compelling that the readers, once started, will not put it down until they've read those beautiful words The End.)

Indicating how much time has elapsed between scenes can be handled very simply by writing: A few hours later, two months later, it was spring again, etc.

Tip #65. In the beginning (of most chapters), there was exposition.

We've discussed how important it is to understand point of view and the function of point of view characters. Sometimes, as the author, you want to pass along to your reader information that will set the scene and create an ambience and mood. And this is general information that relates to the setting, the plot, and character background.

The best place to do this is in the opening paragraphs of a chapter or a scene. Do this quickly, succinctly then introduce your point of view character and get on with the action and/or plot line of your novel.

Remember: Times and readers have changed. Several decades ago, readers would permit a writer to take 5 to 10 pages to establish a novel's setting, characters and major plot line. Today, readers are strongly influenced by both the current frenzied life pace and television. Today, especially in commercial fiction, readers want to get into the main storyline as swiftly as possible. This means you can't dawdle. Set the scene and mood as quickly and economically as possible—both from the standpoint of word count and detail. Introduce your characters and get on with it.

Tip #66. What size do you take in a flashback?

Flashbacks come in three sizes—long, medium and short. They each serve different functions.

Fiction today sometimes begins with a prologue—a scene crammed with drama and action that may occur midway or even further in the book. This scene is introduced as the book's opening to pique the reader's interest, to engage the reader's emotions and to get the book off to a fast start. Once that's accomplished, the writer flashes back to the beginning of the story and tells it in chronological order. The result is that the major portion of the novel is told in one long flashback.

Medium-length flashbacks are usually one to two chapters in length and are often used to give background. For example, say you have a scene in which control of a family business switches from the father to the oldest son as the result of a massive and vicious power struggle. During the struggle, you may use a flashback lasting a chapter or two to depict the beginning of the conflict between father and son years earlier which led to the current confrontation. You must always keep these as brief as possible so that they don't slow the forward momentum of your plot.

Short flashbacks are wonderful tools for revealing character. These are basically brief flashes of memory in which the character remembers something relevant to what's happening in the present. These can be used to explain why a character is behaving in a certain way. They are non-invasive in that they don't disrupt the pace or forward movement of the story nor do they jar the reader out of the story world you've worked so hard to create.

Tip #67. A trigger is not merely part of a gun.

Regardless of its length, the transition into and out of the flashback must be smooth. That trigger can be an event (a graduation ceremony—the character remembers her own graduation years earlier), an incident, a smell, an object of some type (a falling autumn leaf reminds him of autumn years ago) an overheard conversation. Whatever triggering mechanism you use, the bottom line is that it must make sense and be believable that your transitional device would inspire this particular memory to this particular character.

PENCIL SHARPENER #1: Take your favorite book out again and skim through it until you find two or three transitions and two or three flashbacks. Notice how this author handles them.

PENCIL SHARPENER #2: The scene is a party in a ballroom. One element of the party—the party streamers, one particular song, a table decoration, a piece of jewelry one of the characters is wearing, the fragrance of a flower or a food or a perfume—triggers a memory. Write the passage in which the character becomes aware of the element, the moment when the memory is triggered, the item that draws the character back to the party or the present. For example, a man walking down a street in a northern city sees an autumn leaf, he remembers walking down a similar street one autumn years earlier when the leaves had turned red and gold. He's crossing a street, deeply engrossed in his memory. He doesn't see a car turning the corner and the driver honks his horn bringing the man back to the present. What triggers him? What does he remember? What brings him back to the present?

_____

_____

_____

_____

_____

_____

_____

_____

_____

_____

_____

_____

_____

_____

_____

_____

_____

_____

_____

_____

_____

_____

_____

CHAPTER 9: FINAL (W)RITES AND OTHER ET CETERA

There are two times to revise. **First:** As you go along. **Second:** After you've written those two glorious words The End. (Realizing always, with regard to the latter, that you're not really finished even after the book is published because of promotion and marketing.)

In either of the first two instances, don't rush to revise. Divide your work period each day so that you begin by creating new material. When you're tiring and not feeling as fresh and creative as you did at first, put the new material away.

But you're not through.

Now take out the copy you wrote last week and revise it. From this distance in time, you have the emotional objectivity to see its flaws and strengths. Now is when you insert the words you omitted because you couldn't think of them when you were in the heat of creativity.

- Check the spelling.
- Check and correct your punctuation.
- Read for content.
- Check the order of the sentences in your paragraphs.
- Check the order of your paragraphs and your scenes and your chapters.
- Check to be sure each chapter ends with a hook to lure the reader into the next one.

Revise as you go and you'll make it much easier for yourself when you've finished the first draft. If you don't, you may find yourself overwhelmed by the work yet to be done. And you may never get around to the final editing.

Tip #68. Does your title tell the real story?

I know, I know. You've been told the publisher will change your title anyway so why bother? There are several valid reasons why you should get as perfect and appropriate a title as possible.

First: Your title can help sell the book if it's intriguing and makes a favorable first impression on the agent or editor.

Second: If your title tells that first reader (the agent or editor) exactly the type of book it is and what the book is about, it saves that reader's time and avoids confusion. And don't underestimate the importance of saving the reader's time or of titles. Both are important. They do help sell your book.

Assignment: From now on when you're in a bookstore, don't just glance at the cover art. Really see it. Why were you drawn to that cover? Was it the color? The design? The typography? And read the blurbs. Study the titles as well. Do the blurbs and the title do their jobs—do they attract your attention and draw you into the book? Do they tell you what it's about and what kind of book it is?

Tip #69. Eschew obfuscation.

Never write down to a reader. Readers are not dumb. Readers 'r us!

But don't write over our heads, either. If you use too many over-sized and obscure words, you defeat your purpose. You draw attention away from the story you are telling onto yourself. You're saying, "Look at me. See how smart I am and how many big words I know." However, you must also know your audience and their levels of intelligence and education.

Readers don't care how smart you are.

Honest.

They just want a good story.

Now's the time to go through and make sure those big, 99-cent words really belong there.

Bottom Line: Can you say it more simply without losing the story's color and originality?

Tip #70. Check for lazy, do-nothing characters.

When you make your final revisions, force each character to justify his or her presence. Never include a character just because you think he's interesting. Every single character must serve an essential function in the book, must play an important role. If you can tell the same story without that character, take him out.

Can you combine any? If you have a mailman named Pete in chapter two and a mailman named Fred in chapter nineteen, why go to all the trouble to create and describe two characters when one can do the job? Obviously, this doesn't just apply to characters who are doing the same type of work.

Tip #71. Check for go-nowhere scenes, too.

As you re-read your manuscript, study each scene. It must forward the plot. That's absolutely essential. But well-written, thoughtfully planned scenes will also reveal character and emotion. Each scene must add something to your book, must earn its place. Again the litmus test is whether the book will work, it will be understandable without this particular scene. If the book will work, if it makes sense without the scene, dump it.

It's easy to fall in love with our work, to write a scene that sings. Or to create a character so zany and unbelievably cute and clever that we adore him. But we've gotta be tough and professional. The professional writer always keeps in mind the welfare, the quality of the entire book. Don't throw those characters and scenes away. Save them. Use them in short stories. Or create another novel around them. But don't use them where they don't belong.

Tip #72. Does your protagonist still have blue eyes?

As you make your last trip through the pages of your tome, check to be sure that if your hero was driving a Honda Civic in chapter one, he's driving the same car in chapter nineteen. Unless, of course, he sold it and you told the reader.

Check the physical characteristics of each character. Check the time line. Do you move forward in a straight line with only brief flashbacks or do you go backwards and forwards in time? Straight forward is better.

Remember: Your goal is to communicate with your readers and to tell your reader a story—not to dazzle them with stylistic, verbal pyrotechnics.

Tip #73. Last chance checklist.

Now's the time to read through to make sure your nouns are descriptive (not a house—a bungalow, mansion, condo, shack); your verbs must be specific and colorful (not walked—strode, paced, stumbled) and intriguing. Every adjective and adverb must be essential to the sense of the story. "Ly" words can really slow a story.

If you doubt this, read your story aloud, scene by scene, first with the adverbs and adjectives and then without them.

Be honest, be professional. Which sounds better?

Now's also the time to check for unnecessary repetitions. If you told us Harry had polio when he was a child in chapter four, there's no need to tell us again in chapter thirteen. We're not stupid. We'll remember—especially if you've made Harry a character we care about. (You do your job, we readers will do ours.)

Check for unnecessary words. Very, some, now, then, but and just are major offenders. Verbs are sneaky, too. Edit expressions such as "he was standing" to read "he stood."

Check for those pesky exclamation points. If you have to use an exclamation point to generate excitement or to cue the reader that he should be excited, you haven't done your job! Take them out! Immediately! No fooling!

Since this is your last chance checklist, read the opening scene again. Remember, if it doesn't absolutely enthrall your first reader, you won't sell the book.

Ask yourself: Can I make this opening scene more intriguing?

If not, so be it.

If you can, back to the keyboard!

Read your ending one last time. Will it satisfy the reader? Do the hero and heroine get their just desserts? Will the reader be satisfied with the villain's punishment? Have you tied up all the loose ends, unanswered questions? Again, if the answer to any of the questions is no, it's back to the computer.

And one more time: Always submit your very best work. You seldom get a second chance to submit to an editor so never send anything less than your very, very best.

PENCIL SHARPENER: To sharpen your writer's wit, take a favorite scene from a favorite author (other than yourself, of course). Type that scene or at least three or four typewritten pages of it. Be brutal. Cut excess words. Check the verbs and nouns—could you use a more descriptive verb or noun? Could you tighten the dialogue without losing the sense of it? What about adjectives and adverbs? Is each adverb, each adjective appropriate and aabsolutely essential? Or can it be omitted and perhaps strengthen the passage? Are the sentences in the right order? Can they be rearranged to strengthen the impact? What about the paragraphs? Could the order of the paragraphs be revised? Have you followed the natural order of the events? You'll learn a lot about editing your own work, but by using someone else's work, you don't have the same emotional investment so you'll be more objective. Now apply what you've learned to your own work.

NOTES:_____

_____

_____

_____

_____

_____

_____

_____

_____

_____

_____

_____

_____

_____

_____

_____

_____

_____

_____

_____

_____

_____

_____

CHAPTER 10: ONE LAST REMINDER ABOUT EDITS...

Tip # 74. The 12 Commandments of Effective Revision, or The End (sigh!)...is just the beginning.

To a writer, the two most beautiful words in the English language are unquestionably The End. (Not "I do" as some romance writers would have you believe!) Unfortunately, with few exceptions) typing The End is just The Beginning of the final process and the first step in that final process is often painful. However, before even beginning the final revision process, you must establish emotional distance. Celebrate the completion of your novel and then, hard as it may be, put the manuscript away. Keep it out of sight and out of mind for at least two weeks—while you plan or work on your next masterwork. This may be one of the hardest things you'll ever have to do as a writer. You're so thrilled to have the d----d thing done you want to send it off to an agent or editor immediately. However, at this point you must look at your book objectively, as a product not The Great American Novel. Only then can you begin the revision process. Once you've reached that stage, the following 12 commandments will enable you to whip your product into a commercially viable commodity.

1. Thou shalt eschew typographical and grammatical errors. Think about it: Chances are good you will never meet the editors and agents face-to-face. As a result, your manuscript represents you as well as your work. If your manuscript is sloppily prepared and presented, why should that editor or agent trust that you are a professional? This is one place where family and friends can be of inestimable help. Let them read your work specifically for typographical, spelling, and grammatical errors.

2. Thou shalt check thy verbs and nouns. Read through your manuscript paying special attention to every single verb and noun. Make sure each is as colorful and precise as possible. Nothing kills a manuscript quicker than the constant repetition of walk, sit and look. If a character must cross a room, let him amble, stagger, stumble. A character doesn't just live on a street. Drag out your thesaurus. (Personally, I adore Rodale's Synonym Finder.) It will tell your reader about your character, i.e., economic level, taste, pride or lack of pride of place.

3. Thou shalt check the consistency of thy descriptions. If your heroine has blue eyes in chapter 3, make sure her eyes aren't brown in Chapter 17. Take a sheet of paper or create a document on your pc and every time a character is introduced for the first time, make note of the page and chapter number and for each time the character reappears. Then, when you're doing your final revision, you can check the consistency of the descriptions. Same thing for cars and clothes. If you hero wears a Brooks Brothers suit to work in Chapter 5, make sure he wears a similar suit to work in Chapter 12 unless it's a holiday. In that case, why is he working?

4. Thou shalt make a map. Consistency is one of the foundations of good fiction. That's because of the unwritten contract between you, the party of the first part a/k/a the writer, enter into with the party of the second part a/k/a the reader. This means the reader doesn't necessarily believe the fictional world you've created, he just doesn't disbelieve it. Your part of the contract is to write so credibly that he is able to accept your world while he's reading your book.

5. Thou shalt create a calendar. If you take a moment to consider how important time is in our real world today, you will appreciate how important it is in your fictional world for that world to be believable. Why? Harken back to commandments/tips 3 and 4. Consistency. Consistency. Consistency. Create a calendar while you are planning your book and make sure you plot every event on that calendar so you can keep the action moving forward. Yes, you can have flashbacks, but keep them brief and make sure your reader easily understands that's what they are.

6. Thou shalt read thy dialog and make it sing. Remember that fictional dialog does not replicate actual conversation. We are incredibly boring. (If you doubt this, turn on your cell phone's recorder and capture 15 to 20 minutes of real conversation, then try to transcribe it. Or even listen to it! Yawn. Big gaping yawn.) To avoid this, read your dialog aloud. Listen and delete unnecessary words. See if you can make it more relevant by adding an expression or phrase that more clearly delineates that character's background.. A TV reporter, for example, will refer to B-roll, establishing shots. A mechanic may refer to a gummed up carburetor.

7. Thou shalt economize on characters whenever possible. This commandment is most appropriately applied to secondary or tertiary characters. For example, if you have two or three waitresses at the same restaurant and they all have dialog, why not combine them into one? That way you can develop her more fully and make her a person instead a piece of scenery. Do the same for postmen, police officers, sales clerks, etc.

8. Thou shalt eschew obfuscation. Never confuse your best friend, your reader. Reread your manuscript and make sure everything is easily understandable (unless the confusion is a plot twist and even then, remember to foreshadow so your reader does not feel cheated). Any time the reader has to stop and figure something out whether it's garbled dialog, an awkward and abrupt transition or characters with similar-sounding names, you jar the reader out of your fictional world. Not only is it difficult to draw the reader back in, this is an excellent place for the reader to put your book down to finish another day. Your goal should always be to write a book so seamless, so well-paced with characters so finely drawn that the reader, if necessary, will stay up all night to reach your denouement.

9. Thou shalt make haste wisely. Your book cannot "creep" along, and additionally, you must avoid monotony and predictability. 1) Make sure each scene moves the plot forward and contains new information. If it doesn't, be brutal. Dump it! Think of unnecessary scenes as breading on an excellent filet mignon. 2) Be aware that each scene has a tone or a color. It's either physical with lots of action, cerebral with your point of view character mostly thinking or emotional or argumentative, chatty. But (3), be careful not to fall into a predictable rhythm.

10. Thou shalt eschew excess verbiage. Life is filled with repetition. Fiction can't afford it. Again, be brutal and think of breading that filet. Excess verbiage weakens the strength of your writing and also slows it down. Common villains include but are not limited to: but, just, very, so, also, and some. And while we're thinking about it, check your sentences to see if they can be restructured and shortened. Edit and rewrite sentences beginning with there, was or it was.

11. Thou shalt begin and end once again. As Mickey Spillane once said, "Nobody reads a mystery to get to the middle. They read it to get to the end. If it's a letdown, they won't buy your next one. The first page sells the first book. The last page sells the next book." And that is why at this crucial point, you take an objective look at the your beginning and ending. Do they do the job? Are they as dynamic and intriguing as you can make them? If not, back to the computer.

12. If in doubt, thou shalt not send it out. In Sue Grafton's keynote speech several years ago at *Sleuthfest*, the Florida Mystery Writers' of America annual conference, the best-selling author explained that perhaps the worst mistake writers of all ages (and we're talking experience here, not chronological years) is to send out a manuscript before it's ready. The haste is understandable because we are always excited and elated when we finish a book. We want to see it in print NOW! But that's neither smart nor professional. Take your time and make sure your work's as good as you can make it because if you send it out before it's ready, you rarely have the opportunity to darken that agent's email again. (Agents and editors have very good memories!)

In an interview in the May 1954 issue of the Paris Review, Ernest Hemingway shared words about writing fiction that are extremely relevant:

Paris Review:	How much rewriting do you do?
Hemingway:	It depends. I rewrote the ending to A Farewell To Arms, the last page of it, 39 times before I was satisfied.
Paris Review:	Was there some technical problem?
Hemingway:	Getting the words right.

NOTES:＿＿＿＿＿＿＿＿＿＿＿＿＿＿＿＿＿＿＿＿＿＿＿＿＿＿＿＿＿＿＿＿＿＿＿

＿＿＿＿＿＿＿＿＿＿＿＿＿＿＿＿＿＿＿＿＿＿＿＿＿＿＿＿＿＿＿＿＿＿＿＿＿＿＿

＿＿＿＿＿＿＿＿＿＿＿＿＿＿＿＿＿＿＿＿＿＿＿＿＿＿＿＿＿＿＿＿＿＿＿＿＿＿＿

＿＿＿＿＿＿＿＿＿＿＿＿＿＿＿＿＿＿＿＿＿＿＿＿＿＿＿＿＿＿＿＿＿＿＿＿＿＿＿

＿＿＿＿＿＿＿＿＿＿＿＿＿＿＿＿＿＿＿＿＿＿＿＿＿＿＿＿＿＿＿＿＿＿＿＿＿＿＿

＿＿＿＿＿＿＿＿＿＿＿＿＿＿＿＿＿＿＿＿＿＿＿＿＿＿＿＿＿＿＿＿＿＿＿＿＿＿＿

＿＿＿＿＿＿＿＿＿＿＿＿＿＿＿＿＿＿＿＿＿＿＿＿＿＿＿＿＿＿＿＿＿＿＿＿＿＿＿

＿＿＿＿＿＿＿＿＿＿＿＿＿＿＿＿＿＿＿＿＿＿＿＿＿＿＿＿＿＿＿＿＿＿＿＿＿＿＿

＿＿＿＿＿＿＿＿＿＿＿＿＿＿＿＿＿＿＿＿＿＿＿＿＿＿＿＿＿＿＿＿＿＿＿＿＿＿＿

＿＿＿＿＿＿＿＿＿＿＿＿＿＿＿＿＿＿＿＿＿＿＿＿＿＿＿＿＿＿＿＿＿＿＿＿＿＿＿

＿＿＿＿＿＿＿＿＿＿＿＿＿＿＿＿＿＿＿＿＿＿＿＿＿＿＿＿＿＿＿＿＿＿＿＿＿＿＿

＿＿＿＿＿＿＿＿＿＿＿＿＿＿＿＿＿＿＿＿＿＿＿＿＿＿＿＿＿＿＿＿＿＿＿＿＿＿＿

CHAPTER 11: TO MARKET, TO MARKET

First, you must know what you're trying to sell. Is your book literary, mainstream, genre? And there are categories within categories called sub-genres. For example, within mysteries you'll find cozies, police procedurals, historicals, hard boiled, noir to name a few. And then you must know the names of the agents who buy your type of book, and the publishers and the editors at the publishing houses.

Author Jan Burke was a guest speaker at a past meeting of the Florida Chapter of the Mystery Writers of America. At the conclusion of her talk, she asked members to take out pens and pencils and a piece of paper. Then she instructed everyone to write the names of five agents who specialize in representing mystery writers, the names of five each of publishing houses who publish hard cover and paperback mysteries, and five editors who look for and acquire mysteries.

Can you do that for your material? If not, set it as a goal. Whatever your category, know who's selling, buying and publishing it.

Learn everything you can about the publishing industry. *Publisher's Weekly* and *Publisher's Lunch* both offer free, online newsletters that are very informative. To subscribe, go to www.publishersweekly.com and www.publisherslunch.com.

Tip #75. Who's buying what?

Common sense tells you there's no point in trying to sell a domestic problem novel to Cliffhanger Press, a publisher specializing in mystery and suspense. It's also not enough to study *The Writer's Market* and *The Writer's Handbook*, and Jeff Herman's *Guide to Book Publishers, Editors and Literary Agents 2017: Who They Are, What They Want, How to Win Them Over.*

You must strive to read as many books in your field as possible. But don't just read these books, study them. And read as a writer, not a reader. That's the only way you can see precisely what is being published. And while you're reading, make note of the names of the publishers. And don't turn your nose up at small presses or PODs (Print on Demand). In the new millennium, small presses offer wonderful opportunities to beginning and midlist authors.

Publishing has changed drastically. Mergers and acquisitions have severely limited the number of publishers to whom you can submit your material. And more and more, the large publishers are only interested in big names and quick profits. The small presses may not pay the high advances, but you will get your work out there and build your readership. In addition, quite a few are handled by the important book distributors and they will treat you and your work fairly. So, in addition to the books listed above, be sure to check out *The International Directory of Little Magazines & Small Presses* published by Dustbooks. Their website is www.dustbooks.com.

It's also an excellent idea to make contact with someone who either works in or owns a bookstore. These people attend the booksellers conventions. They know who's looking for what. A bookstore contact can be an invaluable source of insider information and, in some instances, contacts as well.

How else can you find out who's buying what? Join different writers groups online. Listen and lurk and ask your questions. You'll find many just by going to your search engine such as Google or Yahoo. Lurk, listen for a while and decide for yourself which are the most relevant and helpful to you.

Tip #76. Simultaneous submissions are not always taboo.

Selling a novel can take a long time. For new authors, the process oftentakes a minimum of six to eight months from the time the manuscript is first submitted to an editor for consideration until the signing of the contract.   It usually takes two to three months even to get rejected.

While magazine writers develop cauliflower ears from being told so many times that simultaneous submissions are out of the question, the novelist learns simultaneous submissions are almost essential. Otherwise, it can take quite literally years to sell one novel. And although most publishers are not thrilled by the idea, most will consider your work even if it is at other houses. However, they do expect to know.

Tip #77. Give the editors what they want.

Some editors—and these are in the minority—want to see the complete manuscript. Others want to see only a query letter which should be single-spaced, run not much longer than two pages and include a brief synopsis of the plot and your background as a writer. Some want to see a query letter and the first three chapters. Still others want to see a synopsis and the first three chapters.

Bottom line: Editors know how they work best. They won't buy a book from a midlist or new author without seeing the whole manuscript, but they know what they want to see initially. Find out what this is (see next tip) and give it to them.

Tip #78. Approaching editors by telephone is not a mortal sin, but almost…

An excellent way to find out what an editor wants to see is to telephone the publishing house. However editors at major publishers are no longer as accessible to new writers as they once were. This means you won't ruin your career by calling, but chances are you won't accomplish much. If you feel you must, then go ahead. Begin by asking the telephone operator for the name of the editor who acquires your type of materials. However, two rules apply, if and that's a big IF you get through to an editor:

First: At the very beginning of the conversation, you must identify yourself as a professional writer with a completed manuscript.

Second: Be prepared to be brief—even with the telephone operator. Keep in mind that you want two pieces of information:

1. You want the name of the editor (and be sure to get the proper spelling of his or her name) who acquires your type of work at this particular publishing house.

2. You want to know how that editor likes to be approached—complete manuscript, partial (synopsis and sample chapters) or query letter.

Be prepared to pitch your manuscript even during this preliminary telephone call. A miracle may occur. The switchboard operator (especially if she's new) may slip up and not only give you the name of the editor, but put you right through. When this happens, the first question the editor will ask is what your book is about.

Rather than be caught numb of tongue and dead of brain, take the time before you call to write a four or five sentence summary of your novel's plot. Make the summary punchy, pithy and intriguing (but not cute!) and remember you want to stimulate the editor's interest so that he'll ask to see it.

Let the editor control the conversation. When she's through talking, so are you.

Tip #79. Two little words that make a big difference.

No, we're not talking about I do or even The End. These magic words are Requested Material. When you mail your manuscript after talking with the editor, you have a distinct advantage. Even though your manuscript may be unagented and unsolicited, you can address it to a specific editor/human being who is expecting it. You'll bypass the mail clerk/receptionist/first reader routine. It's important to mark "Requested Material" on the envelope just to be safe.

Tip #80. Approaching editors and agents at writers' conferences is not injurious to your health or career, but be prudent.

Should you?

Absolutely! That's why they're there.

However, respect their privacy and their time. It's not a good idea to interrupt their meals or conversations. Bide your time, wait until they are alone or attend a session they've taught and approach them afterward or at one of the informal get-togethers.

Some conferences are even so well-organized that staff members are assigned to schedule appointments for these folks.

And save yourself some time and trouble. Don't drag along your 600-page manuscript. Neither the agent nor the editor will have time or inclination to read it at the conference. Your purpose here is the same as the telephone call.

First: You want to meet the person and, in this case, find out if he or she handles your kind of material. If not, ask who does at his/her agency or publishing house.

Second: You want to pitch the idea and see if he or she will take a look at your book when back at the office.

Third: You want to know what to send—query letter, synopsis, etc.

Don't be disappointed if editors and agents aren't willing to take your manuscript to read right then. Can you blame them for not wanting to fly back to New York or California carrying 50 or 60 pounds of unsolicited manuscripts? (However, you can have it available on a flash drive. You just never know…)

And when you go for your appointment or corner them after the lecture, be prepared to get to the point. Tell them your name and give them your business card. Jot the name of your novel and the genre on the back of your card. Again, be prepared with a four or five sentence summary of your novel's plot and strong points because the first question they'll ask in person as well as over the telephone is what your book is about.

Tip #81. A synopsis is...

Sometimes an agent or an editor at a publishing house will want to see a synopsis. It is not the same as an outline. A synopsis is the story of your story told in narrative form. You might consider writing it in the present tense as it lends a note of immediacy. In length, it should run from three to ten pages. It briefly introduces the major characters, gives the major locales of the story and the time frame.

Here's an example of a synopsis of a book that has since been published:

Synopsis

A GRAVE INJUSTICE

A 95,000 word paranormal mystery

By Prudy Taylor Board

Dishonored Grave is the story of Corey Harris, a police reporter haunted by the persistent ghost of Karl von Brett—a WWII GI believed to be a Nazi spy. Corey's life is jeopardized when a series of murders rock the small town of Fort Collier, Florida as she investigates von Brett's suicide, which was actually a murder.

Fired from the *Miami Chronicle*, Corey's perilous adventures begin when she moves to Fort Collier into a home she inherits after her grandmother's death. The home is on the grounds of what was the Buckingham Gunnery School in World War II. Henry Dane, her grandmother's friend and prominent local lawyer, is her first visitor. Corey says she has seen soldiers on maneuvers in the street outside her home. Dane scoffs and tells her there haven't been any soldiers stationed in the area since 1946. He jokes that she must be seeing ghosts.

As the days pass, Corey experiences a series of ghostly visitations from a tall blond GI who tells her his name is Karl von Brett. She hears disembodied voices singing World War II ballads accompanied by the odors of strong Turkish tobacco and lilac. She's afraid she's losing her mind because when she was nine, her parents were gunned down in front of her in a local toy store. She has recovered from posttraumatic syndrome disorder, but only after years of counseling.

To prove she isn't crazy, Corey decides to research military records to see if Karl von Brett really existed. She takes a job as police reporter with the *Fort Collier Journal*, where her new boss, Ben Crawford, is forced to hire her by the paper's owner. One of Corey's first assignments is to cover Artie Farnsworth who's accused of beating his wife to death. While still trying to verify the increasingly persistent von Brett's existence, she not only has time lapses when she believes she's with von Brett on the army base, she also hears his voice in her mind guiding her as she searches for the truth.

At the Fort Collier Historical Museum, Corey finds a gunnery school yearbook from 1943, which contains a photo of von Brett. Now that she knows he's real, Corey talks to Dane. Dane was stationed at Buckingham at the same time as von Brett, but Dane says he doesn't remember von Brett. She soon discovers six von Bretts live in Cincinnati, his hometown. She reaches Karl's brother who refuses to tell her anything except that Karl dishonored his family.

When Dane's WWII division holds a reunion in Fort Collier, Dane turns over personal memorabilia to the historical museum for a special display including old issues of *The Flexigun*, the base newspaper and yearbooks. Corey arranges with Sue Henderson, the curator, to go through the new materials. She discovers that when he served at Buckingham, Karl had a girlfriend named Linda Gonzalez McDaniel. Linda is alive, living in Fort Collier and agrees to talk. The morning of their appointment, Linda's body is found in her garage. The death looks like suicide, but the autopsy reveals it's murder. Corey meets Sgt. Earl French, the detective in charge of the murder investigation.

Earlier, while reading the same military yearbook, Corey found a photo of Karl's graduating class. Dane was in the front row. She noticed that while he was in the photo, Karl was not listed among the graduates. Apparently, he died at Buckingham before graduation. When confronted, Dane admits he knew Karl, but the story behind von Brett's death is ugly and he was afraid she'd write an article about it. Dane claims that Karl tried to steal a top-secret technical manual containing schematic diagrams and operating instructions for the Norden bombsight. When the theft was discovered, Karl hung himself in the rec room at the base rather than face a firing squad.

Corey is sure Karl's no spy. Despite Dane's request to leave the story alone and Crawford's misgivings about her sanity, she's determined to find the truth. However, her investigation is further hampered. While covering a fire at the local Coca Cola© plant, she's attacked and ends up in the hospital. Her injuries are not serious, but she's supposed to rest at home. A friend of Linda McDaniel's brings her a diary and a photo album that the murdered woman planned to show Corey. The diary reveals that Linda and Karl were in love and planned to marry, that he smoked Turkish cigarettes known as Ramses, and that he used Pinaud after shave, which smelled like lilacs. Linda never believed Karl committed suicide, but failed to convince his commanding officer to open an official investigation into his death.

Even though gunners who trained with Dane and Karl are attending the reunion. Crawford will not let Corey cover the reunion saying it's not her beat, but actually is convinced she's becoming obsessed with von Brett. She goes anyway and arranges to talk to Tommy Bob Williams and Pedro Barkley. They served with Dane and, according to Linda's diary, knew Karl. When Pedro fails to show up for the appointment, Corey investigates and discovers his body in his hotel room. It appears he's committed suicide. Tommy Bob leaves town in a hurry, refusing to talk to her.

When Corey gets home, she discovers her house has been broken into. She thinks the only missing items are Linda's diary and photo album.

Corey goes back to the historical museum archives. Tucked between the pages of an old yearbook belonging to Dane, she finds a copy of Karl's autopsy. According to the coroner, Karl's body was found in the barracks and the most visible injury was "A two-centimeter mark that encircled his neck, rising as it reached his Adam's apple. The mark did not match the pattern of the rope taken from his neck."

Corey has reached a dead end until a co-worker suggests consulting Dick Adams, a local psychic. Skeptical, Corey agrees. During the séance, Corey goes into a trance and watches helplessly as three faceless soldiers strangle Karl with his belt. Corey collapses and Sue, the friend and co-worker, calls Ben. The relationship between Corey and Ben has changed over the weeks and Ben has admitted to himself that he is in love with her. He takes her home and stays with her while she cries herself to sleep. The next morning, Ben confesses he loves her and she loves him as well. They make love.

Ben goes to work leaving Corey to recuperate at home. As the day passes, she goes over her notes including what she learned at the séance. Gradually, she realizes only the men who murdered Karl knew he was killed in the rec room, then moved to the barracks where the military police find him. She realizes the marks around his throat didn't match the rope because he'd been strangled with his belt, which proved too short when they tried to hang his body from a beam in the barracks.

Dane shows up bearing a gift of expensive scotch, which he insists she share with him. He says Ben told him she was out sick and he just wanted to be sure she's all right. Corey's suspicious and drinks some of the scotch, but dumps the rest into an arrangement of artificial flowers on the table. She is unaware that the scotch is heavily laced with Xanax. This was Corey's prescription, which had been stolen at the same time Linda's books were taken by a thief Dane hired.

Thinking Corey will soon be unconscious, Dane tells her that he, not Karl, was the spy. He was to be paid for stealing the Norden bombsight manual, but when it appeared he'd get caught, he set Karl up. Dane strangled Karl, manipulating Pedro and Tommy Bob so that they helped him move Karl's body and make it look like a suicide.

Dane further explains that Karl was a natural as the fall guy. His parents were German and he spoke fluent German, although he used it only when he called home. Furthermore, Karl wanted to be a writer and jotted notes wherever he went. As further proof of Karl's guilt, Dane convinced the Counter Intelligence Corps on base that when Linda and Karl went to the beach on dates, it was actually a pretense so that, unbeknownst to Linda, he could deliver stolen information to Nazi saboteurs.

At the same time and unknown to Corey and Dane, Artie Farnsworth tries to make a deal with Sgt. French for a lighter sentence by telling him that Dane had hired John Tyrone Black a/k/a Blackjack, muscle from Miami, to kill Linda McDaniel and Pedro Barkley and to rough up Corey. He knows this because he's in the same cell as Blackjack, who'd been arrested for transporting cocaine for a drug dealer. Dane represents the drug dealer and contacted Blackjack through his client.

At Corey's house, Dane pulls her empty prescription bottle from his pocket and tells her that she's going to commit suicide. He explains that everyone in town knows she's been seeing ghosts and behaving irrationally. They'll think she suffered a breakdown as she did when her parents were killed.

When Corey's drink leaks onto the table from the basket of silk daisies, Dane realizes she didn't finish it. He's outraged and tries to strangle her. They struggle. She fights back, but he's very strong. As she's on the verge of losing consciousness, the temperature in the room plummets and the air is heavy with the aromas of tobacco and lilac. Dane pales and backs away as Karl's wraith materializes. He stretches out his huge hand, and squeezes Dane's heart. Dane gasps and slowly dies.

When the police arrive, they are convinced Dane died of a heart attack. Karl kisses Corey farewell, a wispy breath on her cheek. As the book ends, Corey and Ben take the next step in their relationship by moving in together. Dane's funeral is held, but few attend since Corey's story in the paper discredited him. Corey plans a trip to MacDill Air Force Base in Tampa, the first step in clearing Karl's name. His grave has been dishonored far too long.

THE END

Here is a sample of a query letter:

Ms. Jane Smith, Editor
REALLY SPLENDID BOOKS
3789 Main Street
New York, NY 10001

Dear Ms. Smith:

Clytemnestra (Clyde) Colby, the host of a TV cooking show, travels to an exclusive five-star resort on a remote island off Florida's west coast. She stumbles into a web of mystery involving multiple murders, a murder-for-hire scheme targeting Fortune 500 CEOs, and a $25 million war chest. This is the plot of *Murder a la Carte*, the first in a series featuring Clyde as an amateur sleuth. It is finished and runs approximately 90,000 words.

My previous credits include two novels published by Pocket (Blood Legacy) and Leisure Books (The Vow). I know you don't ordinarily consider unsolicited books, but I thought that since I am a published author perhaps you would take a look at the synopsis and perhaps even the first three chapters.

In addition to the two novels, I have had nine nonfiction books dealing with Florida history published. I am qualified to write these books because I worked as assignment editor at two television stations, the NBC and CBS affiliates in Florida as well as working as reporter for the local newspaper . I know about the food business because my family owned a restaurant for many years and I worked there. I am an active member of the Florida Chapter of the Mystery Writers of America and Mensa. For more information about my background, may I invite you to visit my website?

The URL is at the bottom of this page.

I'll look forward to hearing from you and hope you find Clyde so interesting you'll agree to take a look at her story.

Cordially,

(This book has since been published in hard cover.)

Tip #82. An outline is...

An outline in the strictest definition is a breakdown of the plot and is usually done chapter by chapter. It is not the same as the synopsis in that it does not have to be told in a narrative or story form, but spells out the action of the plot. As a suggested length, each chapter should take no more than half of a double-spaced page. And this outline, which is used to sell the book, is not the same as your working outline. The working outline spells out viewpoint character, etc. The selling outline tells the narrative of the novel in a chapter-by-chapter breakdown. If submitted by email, be sure to single space your outline.

Tip #83. A partial is...

Sometimes in your communication with an agent or editor, you'll be asked to provide a partial. This is literary shorthand for a combination of the synopsis and the first three chapters of your manuscript.

As a rule, the agent/editor wants to see chapters one, two and three—not the best three chapters. This is so they can get a sense of your ability to hook the reader's interest in the first chapter and to maintain the pace, tone and continuity of the book. They will ask to see a partial even though you have the entire manuscript completed because they can tell that quickly if they want your book.

Tip #84. Once the publisher sends the contract...

Now is actually a good time to get an agent. If you don't have one, you might ask your editor for the name of several agents he or she deals with on a regular basis. Most don't mind making suggestions because they'd rather deal with agents when it comes to the business end of publishing your book. You might also join a writers' group and ask a published author. Network.

If you can't get or prefer not to have an agent, then have the contract checked out by a lawyer, preferably one who is familiar with the publishing business. Depending on where you live it may be difficult to find such a lawyer, but you can check with your family lawyer or your local bar association or online via the internet.

Now that you've got your contract, it's an appropriate time to celebrate, but the process is just beginning. One of the first disappointments you'll undoubtedly experience is when you learn that it may be one or two years before your book is published. The reason there is such a delay is because book publishers establish their publishing schedules several years in advance. Sometimes but not often, an author will fail to deliver a manuscript on time. In this instance, a slot may open and your editor may push up your publication date.

Between the contract and publication, your book will go through a number of steps. If you submit a completed manuscript, a partial distribution of your advance money will be made when you sign the contract. Another payment will be made when you deliver the manuscript edited to the satisfaction of your editor. Some publishing houses divide the payment into thirds with the third payment due when the book is published.

From the standpoint of the process, once you have delivered the edited manuscript to your editor, start on your next novel the next day because it will be months before you hear again. Then one day, probably when you've given up hope, UPS or FedEx will drop off a package from your publisher. Depending on the publisher and the respect the publisher has for its first-time authors, it will contain either your copy edited manuscript or the galleys. The galleys (this is your manuscript typeset as it will actually appear in print) are sent to you so that, as the author, you have one last chance to check your manuscript for accuracy and to approve the edits and revisions your editor and/or copy editor have made.

About the cover. At some point in this same period, you may receive either preliminary sketches of your cover or copies of the already printed final product. Depending again on the amount of respect the publisher has for its new authors, you may have an opportunity to look at it and make suggestions; however, don't expect your suggestions to be given much weight. Cover art is not considered the province of the young (as in just starting out) novelist.

And about the copyright. The major publishing houses have legal departments who will apply for the copyright. You don't need to worry about that. The only caveat is that you should be sure the novel is copyrighted in your name, but if you are dealing with a reputable publisher that won't be a problem.

If you are concerned, file your own copyright. Write: U.S. Copyright Office, 101 Independence Ave. S.E., Washington D.C. 20559-6000, call (202) 707-3000 or go online and enter www.loc.gov/copyright/.

Tip #85. Getting an agent isn't impossible, it just seems that way.

As suggested earlier, one place to get an agent's name is from an editor who's interested in acquiring your book. There are other places. For example, if you're savvy, you already read all the new releases in your type of material. But do you read the acknowledgments in books? You'll be surprised at how many writers acknowledge their agents in their books.

You can get the agent's address from several different sources—from the telephone book collection at your local library, by calling information, by doing a search online or by checking the Writer's Digest Guide to Agents or your library's copy of Literary Market Place (known as LMP) or Jeff Herman's Guide to Book Publishers, Editors and Literary Agents 2017: Who They Are, What They Want, How to Win Them Over.

It doesn't hurt to telephone the agent's office to check the mailing address and the name of the associate who handles your type of material. You may even get to talk to the agent, but most prefer to be contacted by letter or email first.

In the letter, or email, tell the agent how you got his or her name and why you are contacting him or her as opposed to another agent. In other words, you might tell the agent you have learned that he/she handles historical romances or science fiction or women's or literary fiction, that you have read the works of his or her author, etc. Agents are busy business people. They don't want their time wasted. They really don't want to be contacted by authors who haven't done their own research.

Even if you already have a contract, good agents won't agree to represent you until they've read your book.

Tip #86. What an agent can and cannot do for you.

The services an agent provides will vary from agent to agent. Some like to read your material on a project-by-project basis and deliver it to editors for their consideration, fulfilling their most important role to your career in the negotiation of the contract. Others think in terms of managing your career. The days when agents had the time to line edit your copy is long gone.

Expect the agent to charge 15 percent commission for sales to U.S. publishers and 20 percent for foreign sales. Also you should know that the publisher may pay the agent, the agent will deduct the commission and send you his or her check for the balance.

You should know both what you want from an agent and what that agent will provide before you enter into any sort of professional relationship. How do you find out? You ask questions. First, the agent will look at your work and decide whether or not the agency wants to handle it. But at the same time, you should be asking about the services his or her agency provides and deciding whether they will meet your need on a long-term basis.

Basically, an agent can negotiate the contract with the publisher. More than that, the agent can act as a mediator should problems arise during the publication of the book. The agent is in a much better position to deal with the editor should it come to a question as to the competence of a copy editor, the effectiveness of a cover, the number of author's copies, the amount of promotion/publicity you can expect from the publisher and, of course, the money and subsidiary rights. Should a dispute arise, the editor would much rather deal with the agent who is more objective than the author. More importantly, the agent can then play the role of bad guy and keep the author/editor relationship separate and safe.

What an agent can't do for you is very simple. Regardless of how powerful an agent you acquire, that agent cannot sell a bad book. Or even a good book without commercial or sales potential. In other words, having an agent does not guarantee that your book will sell.

Tip #87. What's a POD?

POD is an acronym for print on demand, a technological development that has revolutionized the publishing industry. Quite literally, it means that a publisher may print the exact number of books ordered ranging from one on up. To you, a beginning writer, publishers using POD offer opportunity because the cost of printing and publishing has gone down making way for the emergence of more small presses. This is wonderful news because as the major publishers acquired

smaller publishing houses, the number of markets where new writers might sell their books shrank. The immediate result was that the responsibility for seeking new talent shifted to agents. However, the agents found—and find—it's easier to sell and promote established authors, so they concentrate on these writers. This leaves the newbie out of the loop. POD provides a means of re-entry via small presses.

There are two types of small presses that utilize this technology. The one is the small press that functions along the lines of the major publishers. You submit the manuscript, the editor either accepts or rejects it. You may or may not be paid a royalty, although if you are it's traditionally less than major publishers pay. You are given a contract and you are paid royalties. Your manuscript is edited by professionals, professionals design the book and the cover art.

The other type is the small press that you pay to publish your book. The fees vary depending on the services the press provides. However, the fee includes the book design, the cover art and the actual production. Whether or not your book is professionally edited depends on the house. If you decide to go this route, make sure that the editors do not just accept any manuscript submitted and that your work is edited—at the very least, copyedited.

There are drawbacks to both. Regardless of the good reputation of the individual small press, these books are still widely—and often unfairly—considered vanity publications although this perception has gradually changed. This means small press books are not reviewed as a rule and it's more difficult for their authors to get publicity. In addition, the author must do his own marketing, although that's typical of even the major publishing houses today when they take on new writers.

There are advantages. The royalties are better, and the author has more control over the book. Plus, major book distributors will handle books published by small presses. Some small presses help writers with the marketing, perhaps not in dollars, but in information. Then there's the speed of production. As indicated earlier, the traditional publisher will take anywhere from one to two years to publish your book. Utilizing POD technology, a publisher can bring books out in an average of four months.

The caveats:

First: Make sure the publisher screens manuscripts. If the company takes any book, it's really a vanity publisher and will have little industry standing regardless of how good your book is.

Second: As with any publishing contract, make sure a lawyer familiar with the publishing industry checks it out. Personally, my book Blood Legacy was reprinted by iUniverse (www.iUniverse.com). I was very satisfied with the final product and found the company and its representatives helpful and professional to work with; however, there are other companies. *21st Century Publishing: An Author's Introduction to Print-on-Demand Book Publishing* by Julie Duffy is an excellent source of information and is available at Amazon.com.

Tip #88. Speaking of Amazon.com…

In addition to traditional publishing and POD publishing through small presses, the industry has seen the emergence of total self-publishing through POD services such as the one offered by Amazon.com, CreateSpace (createspace.com). Total author control. The author formats to the specifications required by the publisher, submits the manuscript, designs and submits the cover art (paper covers only), and orders a proof for review. Additional editing, formatting and design services offered for additional fees. It's even possible to obtain an ISBN number required for all books. This bar code and 11 or 13 digit number identifies the publisher and helps all outlets for sale of the book, identify the particular book. The author sets the price.

Once you approve your book, you can order any amount from one on up. Authors generally pay cost plus shipping. Createspace provides an author site and automatically publishes the book to Amazon.com where readers are able to order at any time.

Royalties are spelled out up front and the author can arrange for automatic deposit to his or her checking account.

Createspace is not the only game in town, either. Smashwords (smashwords.com) is another successful site. There are others, but be sure to do your research.

Word to the wise: While this form of self-publishing offers the absolute quickest way into print, there's no editor at the gate making sure the work is ready for publication. Like everything else in this particular form of publishing, it's all under the control of the author. Make sure you get your book professionally edited and make absolute sure it's the best it can possibly be. There are some incredibly good books published through these services, but there are also some incredibly bad ones published, too. Make sure yours is one of the great ones!

Tip #89. What's an ebook?

Simple. The "e" stands for electronic. The book is stored in cyberspace and, for a fee from which the author's royalties are paid, the book can be downloaded to ebook readers, personal computers, laptops, and some PDAs (a palm-sized digital access device). Depending on the terms of the contract, POD publishers usually make their books available as ebooks as well as print. The ebook has generated an industry of its own with the manufacture of specific readers such as Kindle, The Nook and Rocketbook.

It's important to remember, though, that not all publishers—POD publishers or self-publishing platforms—automatically format an author's manuscript for ebooks. This may mean an additional fee. Sometimes, the author will either format the manuscript himself, or hire someone who formats ebooks professionally.

Tip #90. The appearance of the manuscript does make a difference.

Yes, you've got a great plot. And splendid, breathing characters. Your settings scintillate with vitality and authenticity. So why should the appearance of your manuscript count? Because, for one thing, you've got to make it easy for your agent/editor to read your magnificent marvel.

Remember: You are competing with the best in the business, with the professionals. If your manuscript is laced with typographical errors, it can well lead the agent/editor to assume that you are sloppy in your research or that you are sloppy in your writing style. And that just doesn't cut it in today's tough market.

Your manuscript speaks to your professionalism. You wouldn't go to an important business appointment in your 'jammies and slippers and you shouldn't send your manuscript off to represent you at that appointment looking less than its very best.

Use spell check on your computer. Run the grammar check. You'll have to ignore many of the corrections as not relevant to your style, but the computer will catch gross errors. It's a tedious task so you can make it easier on yourself by checking the manuscript in shorter segments as you go.

Tip #91. Get someone in your support group to read your final draft. (What support group? See Tip #94.)

I know, I know. The blasted thing's done and you want to get it in the mail. However, the worst thing you can do at this point is to rush. Unless, of course, you're pushing a deadline which happens.

Take your time to be sure that every manuscript is as perfect as you can make it. One last time, give it to someone you trust in your support group. Ask that person to read it from front to finish and give you some feedback and check for errors of any type. You don't have to accept the criticism—it's always your book, but one final read-through by an objective and caring person can prevent a blunder and help secure a sale.

Tip #92. How long should you wait to hear from a publisher or an agent?

That, of course, varies. Most publishers take months to make a decision. Which brings us to another function the agent can provide for you—that of nagging. The agent can follow up or nag the editor much more comfortably than the writer can. Quite often, too, it's simpler for the agent who may be following up on several projects with the same editor.

If you're submitting your manuscript without an agent, give the publisher six weeks to six months. Check *Writer's Market* or *Jeff Herman's Guide* (more information on these in the reference chapter) because the publishers' listings tell how long it takes the individual publishers to make a decision.

Tip #93. When you don't hear.

If you initially submit your manuscript via snail mail, you should include a self-addressed postcard. On the back, it should read something like this:

> **This will acknowledge receipt of manuscript entitled**
> **FOOLS RUSH IN**
> **submitted**
> **On** _____ **date by** _____.

The second line above is for the person to sign or initial.

Be sure to make a note of the publisher's name in the return address position on the front of the card. Otherwise, if you make simultaneous submissions, you won't know who's responding.

Your next step, should you not hear within the six weeks to six months, is to write a pleasant business letter telling the editor when you sent the manuscript and ask if he's had a chance to consider it yet. Telephone only if you get no response to your letter within a couple of weeks following your letter.

From here on out, you should follow up in some manner at least once a month, but don't become irritable or demanding. The decision to buy a book seldom rests with one person. Even if the editor reading your manuscript loves it, he's going to have to take it through a number of meetings and generate a lot of support from other editors before a buy decision is made—and that can easily take three to six months.

Remember: Check the website of the agent/editor before sending your initial query and before following up. In this wondrous age of the Internet, agents and editors are generally very clear on their websites as to what they want and what kind of follow up they deem acceptable.

PENCIL SHARPENER: Write your four or five sentence summary of your book here. Make it as interesting and intriguing as possible. Think of it as a 30- to 60-second commercial. _____

_____

_____

_____

_____

_____

_____

_____

_____

_____

_____

_____

_____

_____

_____

_____

_____

_____

_____

_____

_____

_____

Sample cover sheet for your novel manuscript.

(**NOTE:** You want to make the category and proposed length immediately clear to the agent/editor.)

(**NOTE:** If you are represented by a literary agent, you will put your agent's name, address and phone number here instead of your own.)

FOOLS RUSH IN (Place 1/3 of the way down the page)

By Jane R. Doe

A mainstream coming-of-age novel of approximately 100,000 words.

Your name
Your address
Your phone number
Your email address

Format for standard manuscript page.

(**NOTE:** on every single page of your manuscript except the cover sheet, you must include in the upper left corner, a word from the title, your last name and the page number.)

FOOLS RUSH IN

Chapter One

Please notice that your pages are double-spaced and your paragraphs are indented five spaces. Don't use a fancy typeface. Stick with Courier or New Times Roman and 12 point. Adjust the quality of the paper you use to print. Definitely, you should print only on one side of the paper.

Make sure you change your ink cartridge when it runs low. A cleaner and darker manuscript will help create a more professional impression. Put yourself in the editor's place. Day in and day out, editors read hundreds, thousands of manuscripts. They experience incredible eye strain in the normal course of their work. As a result, they won't even bother with a sloppy manuscript. Make it as easy as possible for them to read and to buy your manuscript. That's just good business. And this is, after all, a business.

Don't justify your margins. Use one-inch margins. Start each chapter on a new page. If this isn't enough information about formatting a manuscript. There are a number of good books published on the subject. Check the catalog of books published by *Writer's Digest*.

CHAPTER 12: SURVIVAL TECHNIQUES

One of the most important caveats following your first sale: Don't assume your second sale will be easy. Until you've sold four or five books, it will still be difficult. That's because it will take time to build a readership and to prove to your publisher that you can produce manuscripts on deadline and of consistent quality. You can't slack off. Many excellent careers have been dashed on the pages of a second novel that didn't live up to the promise of the first.

And also, don't berate yourself if you don't get a huge advance. It's true, there are advantages to big advances. If a publisher invests a lot of money in a first novel, you can be sure that company will allocate substantial monies for promotions and publicity. However, if that first novel doesn't earn back the advance, the author quickly loses his or her luster in the eyes of the acquisitions editor. Think about it. Unfortunately, for the most part, the successful editor in today's major publishing houses is lauded when he brings in books that make a profit. The higher the profit, the greater the editor's job security.

Tip #94. You don't have a support group? You should and here's how to start one.

Attend every writers' conference your budget will allow. While you're there, make it a point to touch base with every writer from your hometown or easily accessible surrounding geographical area. Post a message on the conference bulletin board informing other writers you want to start a writers' group. At home, run a little classified ad in the weekly shopper or a personal in your daily if cost isn't out of sight. Do an online search for local groups. Two things to keep in mind:

First: You're probably better off not meeting in people's homes if possible because it's sometimes difficult to keep things moving forward and to maintain a businesslike atmosphere.

Second: You need pre-agreed-upon guidelines for critiquing which is why you're meeting. Guidelines also prevent disputes.

So as far as a meeting place is concerned, most libraries and many bookstores welcome writers' groups. And there's usually no charge for a nonprofit group. Some restaurants have meeting rooms where they'll let you meet. Or a member may have access to a clubhouse where she or he lives.

Critiquing is an art and this is where you need to tread carefully if you don't want to create hard feelings that will rend the group in twain. Balance is the answer. While most writers are desperate to hear the truth (how can I fix it if I don't know what's wrong), they are also insecure. The solution is to tell the truth about the manuscript's problems, but always begin with what's well written before you critique the weaknesses. A worthwhile goal is to attempt to find some aspect of the writing to praise for every area that needs work. This is often an unattainable goal, but keeping it in mind will help you be even in your criticism.

Also establish time limits—including a beginning and ending time for the meeting. If your group is small, ten pages is a good limit. If your group is larger, five is better unless someone's on deadline or there's extra time. Everyone brings something to be critiqued and either e-mails it to members ahead of time or brings enough copies so that each member can have one in front of them. Make it clear that the comments are only suggestions and the writer should neither spontaneously accept nor dismiss them, but think about them for several days before deciding if they have merit.

Whether or not you charge dues is an individual matter, but this can limit the meeting places available to you since libraries often don't lend meeting rooms to for-profit groups. Having officers is not necessary unless you are going to structure yourself as an organization and plan on bringing in guest speakers, etc. For an informal critique group, it's usually enough to have a different chairman for each meeting.

Tip #95. Getting the most out of your critique group.

These are such handy-dandy tips that we've included a copy in the back of the book so that you can easily copy them for your critique group.

1. Be on time.

2. What another person chooses to write is his or her choice. Whether or not you agree with what they've written doesn't matter. Content is not up for discussion.

3. A good critique concerns the following:

   • Does the plot move?
   • Are the characters well-defined?
   • Did the writer use the correct tense?
   • Are there any grammatical glitches that caught your eye?
   • Do you like the story?
   • Did it hold your interest?

4. Offer positive suggestions for how something could be revised to improve any of the above.

5. If the group members who have offered critiques before you have said what you would say, don't repeat it. It's perfectly acceptable to state that you agree with what's been previously said. Add only comments that haven't already been said. Make sure you've written your comments on the manuscript so that the writer can review them later.

6. As the writer, offer a BRIEF explanation of your piece before reading. It should only be a paragraph at the most and should contain whether or not your piece is part of a larger work and what, if anything, you'd like to do with it—submit it to a magazine? A blog article? Just for fun?

7. As the writer, take the comments of the critiquing member as suggestions, not required revisions. Your voice is always the one that counts. Seriously consider each suggestion, but the final decision is yours.

8. Do NOT defend or explain your work after someone offers a critique. The best answer is, "Thank you." If you don't understand what the person means, definitely ask for an explanation.

9. If you've revised a piece, you should be able to bring it back for further input, so bring it back to read again.

10. Develop a thick skin and enjoy the process. The group must be supportive and dedicated to improving its members' writing skills. The wider world can be a cruel place for writers. Every reader has an opinion and not everyone is nice about it. If you end up publishing, you'll end up with a nasty review sooner or later and the self-confidence you develop in this group will be your best defense.

Tip #96. Start your own writing textbook.

From now on when you read a passage in another author's book that really works, make a copy or cut it out and file it away for reference. *No!* You are not being encouraged to plagiarize another writer's work, but to figure out what *your* writing weaknesses are and learn from the writers who handle these well.

Get one of those big notebooks with several sections. Label sections for setting, character, dialogue, transitions, dreams, symbolism—whatever. It's your notebook. And when you read a passage of dialogue that strikes you as being especially effective, photocopy a page or so and paste it in your workbook. Then when you're working on a project and you're stumped, go to your workbook to see how a pro handled it.

A writer friend of mine was writing a dream sequence and it just wasn't working. She referred to her workbook and, by reading dream scenes written by other writers, she realized hers wasn't working because she had been so busy describing the landscape of the dream that she had failed to include the emotion of the dreamer.

Tip #97. Learn from every mistake, every rejection.

At first, you'll receive only printed rejections. As you grow increasingly proficient, the quality of your rejections will improve. When editors start to write letters telling you what was wrong you are **ON THE VERGE!** Celebrate these rejection letters.

If you're really determined, you'll take the next step. You'll read these letters with a truly open mind. You don't have to agree with everything the editors write, but consider the points they make. And, if you do get a really helpful letter, sit right down and write that editor a thank you note. But keep it brief and be sincere.

Tip #98. When is a rejection not really a rejection.

If ever you receive an extremely detailed rejection letter in which the editor has taken the time and trouble to spell out precisely why she rejected your manuscript, rejoice. What that editor is really hinting is that if you make the revisions she suggests, she'll *possibly* take another look at your manuscript. She won't come right out and request that you make these revisions because she does not want to be obligated. She doesn't know you or your work and she can't be sure that you can revise the manuscript to suit her needs.

So here's what you do. As always, study her suggestions carefully. Make as many of them as you feel you can live with, then write her again. Thank her for taking the time to give your manuscript such thorough consideration. Explain that you have considered her comments carefully and that you have revised the manuscript incorporating many of her suggestions. Ask her, with this in mind, if she would be willing to take a look at your revised manuscript or at least the first three chapters.

Chances are she'll write back with a go ahead because she's not going to take the trouble to critique a novel she's not at least slightly interested in. If she doesn't, just be grateful for the invaluable assistance she gave you and know that you now have a better book.

Tip #99. Handling rejection without giving up or driving your loved ones crazy.

Handling rejection is the most difficult task any writer must face. There's a technique, which you'll learn, and you can do it!

First: To keep from going crazy, start another book or writing project at once. You should have two or three in the works anyway because publishers do not like to deal with one-book authors. The lore in publishing is that publishers like to develop authors, which means they want someone who is going to write a lot of books. In today's market, it more often happens that they are going with the known and renowned rather than building careers, but ideally, they will talk to you about other projects as soon as they've purchased the one book, so be ready and have something to offer. (And even if they don't buy your second novel, you are now a professionally published author and that gives you an ingress to sell the second novel that you didn't have with the first.)

Second: Give yourself a specified amount of time to mourn, feel frustrated, angry and unappreciated. But don't make it too long—two or three hours is usually enough. During that time, cry, stomp your feet, pound your head against the wall, curse—do whatever it takes (as long as its legal and not destructive) to work through the emotion.

Third: Re-read the rejection letter and see if it has value. If the pointers are helpful, start immediately to make the recommended revisions.

Finally: Get the manuscript back out in the mail as soon as possible. As long as it's somewhere in the mail or on a desk, you have hope—and that hope is what is what will keep you writing.

Most important: Don't ever have all your writing eggs in one basket. Always have a work in progress.

Tip #100. Don't give up your day job!

This tip is not meant to discourage you by any means, but novel writing is a business involving sales. Translated that means you will have to sell three or four books and begin to build up a following before you will get the kind of advances and/or royalties to enable you to quit your job. There are exceptions, but for the majority of writers this is the truth about novel writing. We don't get the six-figure advances for our first books. We have to build our new career as if it were a new business. Which, of course, it is. With that in mind, don't give up your job or make major expenditures after you've signed the contract on your first novel.

As you begin work on your novel, it's hoped the information contained in these pages will be helpful to you. Don't get discouraged. Enjoy the writing, the process of writing and persevere. Few joys compare to that of selling your first novel—except perhaps holding your newly published book in your hands and knowing that you did it!

NOTES:_____

_____

_____

_____

_____

_____

_____

_____

_____

_____

_____

_____

_____

_____

_____

_____

_____

_____

_____

CHAPTER 13: PRE-PUBLICATION MARKETING

You've studied the first part of this book until the pages are worn. Your manuscript is finally done and you're starting to send it out to agents and editors hoping one will want it and put you on the bestseller's list. Now what? Do you start writing your next book? Sure.

But hold on a minute, you aren't quite finished with this one. Now comes the fun part: We write the books in solitude and when we finish, we're forced out of our caves and away from our laptops to try to convince the public to buy our book.

Gone are the days when publishers did all the marketing and booked their authors into book tours and speaking engagements on television and radio stations. Unless you're J.K. Rowling or Stephen King, you're on your own.

Of course, if you've got an unlimited budget, you can hire a firm that specializes in author and book publicity. For prices ranging from $2,500 per month up into the stratosphere, these firms can get you national exposure for you and your book.

These tips are written for the rest of us. The struggling writers who enjoy writing more than marketing, but realize that without readers buying our books, all of our efforts will just sit on a shelf.

Marketing doesn't have to be expensive or difficult. It will take some time, though, and it's up to you to decide how much, or how little, to do. Remember that not every tip will work for every writer or every book.

Ideally, you started working to establish an on line presence way before typing "The End." If not, don't despair, it's never too late.

Tip #101. Brand Yourself.

Who are you? What type of books do you write? If you can stick to one genre in your writing, say mysteries, for example, you can establish yourself as a mystery writer. Every time someone sees your name on a book cover, they know what to expect—an action-packed mystery with a twist at the end. Your name becomes your brand and helps sell every book you write.

If you write in several genres, your task is harder, but not impossible. Strive to deliver the best possible product every time and, even though the genre may differ, a prospective reader will know a book with your name on the cover is worth the price. You should also consider a nom de plume for the second genre so that your readers won't be confused.

Tip #102. Oh, No. Not the Internet!

It's inevitable these days that the Internet and social media have to be a part of branding yourself and establishing your platform. Why? Because that's where you can reach the most people for the least amount of moolah. Start working on your brand (See Tip #101) as soon as possible. The most successful writers I've seen on social media are those who let the readers into their lives a bit. I'm not suggesting laying everything out there for strangers, but post tidbits about what you're writing. Ask for suggestions on where your characters should go next—Las Vegas or Los Angeles. Run contests where the winner is a named character in your work-in-progress. Have your followers vote on which of two book covers they like best.

Announce the milestones and post pictures to go along with the posts.

"Finished the manuscript!"

"Submitted to the editor!"

"The agent wants it!" With this one, you can post a video of you doing the happy dance.

Once the book is out, do not continually post advertisements. Don't abuse your followers by posting the link several times a week! For example, if your book is about an inspiring mom, it would be a great idea to post a link ahead of Mother's Day annually in addition to posting occasionally through the year, but if you try to post an advertisement once a week, you run the risk of irritating your followers. "Unfollowing," to use the Facebook term, is just a click away—and you've lost a potential reader for the books you have yet to write.

Tip #103. Networking

Writers' conferences and writers' organizations like Mystery Writers of America, Sisters in Crime, The Women's National Book Association, Florida Writers Association, Science Fiction and Fantasy Writers, National Writers' Union, Romance Writers of America and Horror Writers of America to name a few, are the places to go for networking. This list is by no means a complete list of the only groups out there. Simply type in "writers organizations" in your search engine and you'll find local, regional and national groups. Attend meetings armed with business cards. Offer to speak on an aspect of writing that you know well: Do you know how to research historical facts exceptionally well? Are you an expert at formatting for self-publication?

Not only do these types of organizations provide opportunities to socialize and network, they also provide opportunities for education on everything from the craft to the marketing and help connect you with the people who have the answers you need. And don't forget, you may also have just the missing puzzle piece someone else needs.

Tip #104. The Blog

Seriously? All this and now you expect me to write a blog?

Sure! Just remember these guidelines:

1. Keep it short. No one wants to read a 3,000 page essay. Around 500 words or less is perfect.
2. Do all of us a favor and don't write a blog about writing. There are enough blogs on line about the craft of writing that you could never read them all if you had a lifetime.

3. Publicize your blog. Put the address on your business cards. Join blog campaigns and blog hops. A blog hop is where a group of bloggers agree to guest host on each other's blogs. Fun, right?

4. Write about something you love. Find one central theme – the area you live, the types of books you like, pets, gardening, house decorating, holiday tips – and make most of your posts touch on that theme. Most, but not necessarily all. Occasionally, something will touch you and force you to write about it. Just do it.

Tip #105 SEO – huh?

Uh oh. An acronym. Now we're in trouble!

Not really. SEO stands for "Search Engine Optimization" and is not as complicated as it sounds. This has to do with the words you enter on your blog that are searchable on the internet. The words you "tag" will be the ones that will show up when someone searches the internet for a particular topic.

For example, to find an article about The Tarpon Club, a creative aquatics group that used to be active at Florida State University, you could enter "creative aquatics, water ballet, The Tarpon Club, Esther Williams." Now, if anyone types in any of those phrases in the search engine, your blog article will show up.

This is particularly useful when you want to publicize your book. Say you wrote a book about cross-pollination of hibiscus plants. You might want to use the obvious words like "cross-pollination" and "hibiscus," but you could also add in "tropical flowers" and "cross-fertilize."

Tip #106. What's a tagline and why do I need one?

A tagline is a one sentence summary of a book. Best place to research examples are websites like imbd.com. A book tagline is the same as a movie tagline. Here's a few examples from the imbd site:

1. Collide: An American backpacker gets involved with a ring of drug smugglers as their driver, though he winds up on the run from his employers across Cologne's high-speed Autobahn.
2. Punching Henry: Hapless satirical songwriter Henry Phillips is lured to L.A. when a veteran TV producer decides to make a show about the life of a loser.
3. La La Land: A jazz pianist falls for an aspiring actress in Los Angeles.
4. Casablanca: In Casablanca, Morocco in December 1941, a cynical American expatriate meets a former lover, with unforeseen complications.

Tip #107. Book cover design

If your book is being traditionally published, you'll have professional graphic artists and editors working on your book cover. You may or may not be required to provide the text.

If you are self-publishing your book, the book cover is your ball of wax. Go to your bookshelf or the library and pull out several books that you love. Study their book covers carefully. Notice the colors, the font used for the title and other copy printed on the front cover. Notice the placement of the text and the artwork. Turn it on the side and look at the spine to see what information is printed there and how it's presented. Turn it over and study the back cover. Or contact a local publishing firm and talk to their cover artists to find out if any do freelance work.

If you've elected to publish through Createspace or a similar company, they will have published guidelines. You'll have to be concerned with dpi (dots per inch) and margins. If it's in your budget, you may want to come up with the concept and hire a graphic artist, either on your own or through your self-publisher, to finish the design to the required specifications.

Tip #108. The Blurb

Ever notice all the neat comments on book covers from established authors?

"A thrilling ride!" Big-time Mystery Writer Joe Schmo.

"I loved this book!" Big-time Author Rebecca Reader.

How do the authors get those quotes? By asking. If you're trying to get someone like Stephen King or J.K. Rowling to give you a blurb, you may be out of luck. But there are plenty of locally well-known authors who would be happy to read a chapter or two and send you a blurb.

How do you use them? On the back of your book. On a fly-leaf if you've got one. In advertising, on posters, bookmarks—basically anywhere you think might catch a reader's eye.

Why do authors use them? Think of it. You've written what you think is a pretty good book. But it's your first (or second, or third) book and only a handful of people know your name. If you're fortunate enough to obtain a blurb from an author with more name recognition than you, you are also able to perhaps attract some of their readers. "If Big-time Mystery Writer Joe Schmo says this is a good book, it's worth a shot." Of course, that only works once. This is where the previous suggestions to write the best book you possibly can come in to play.

Tip #109. The Marketing Plan

"A plan? Can't I just go hang out in front of the local book shop with a carton of books? Does that count?" Well, no. It doesn't work that way.

"I've been working on my brand and have a great following on social media. Isn't that enough?" No, again.

At the same time you're building an online presence and sharpening your brand, you need a marketing plan.

A marketing plan is a detailed map of how you expect to present your book to the public. It's much easier to get from the garage to your favorite restaurant if you know which roads you're going to take. The following is a sample marketing plan for a young adult fantasy book. Tweak this to suit your genre.

SAMPLE MARKETING PLAN

GOODREADS: You can join as an author and run a giveaway. You set the number of books you're going to give away, you set the number of days people can enter the drawing. Goodreads will send you the name and email of the winner and you need to mail the book out as soon as possible. You can include a personal note thanking them for entering your giveaway and asking them for a review if they're so inclined. That's the end of the contact you have with them. Your book will show up in the giveaway advertisements and sections on Goodreads and will attract some attention. Readers are always surfing for books there so at a minimum, you may get more people reading your synopsis. They may not win your book, they may not run over to your website and buy it right now, but you've put your book in front of them.

There's also a scifi and fantasy book club group on Goodreads with more than 14,000 members. Join it. Don't sell them your book, but when you do a giveaway, post it there. Be careful about placing promotional posts on group pages. Read their rules and follow them. When in doubt, contact the organizer of the group and ask.

REDDIT: Check out the Fantasy Bookclub on reddit. It doesn't look like there's a charge, however, they're recommending books to each other. https://www.reddit.com/r/Fantasy_Bookclub.

MEETUP: Meetup is free to join and there are several gamer groups. Read the descriptions of the groups (including location) and perhaps contact the organizer. Offer a free book to him or her if he'll let you give a presentation about your book to his group. Or, offer to do a drawing for one of your books at the event.

BOOK CLUBS: There's a site called "bookclubreading.com" that will list your book for book club possibilities. I'm not sure of the cost, but that might be a possibility.

LIBRARIES: Once you have your speeches practiced to the point where you feel comfortable, contact local libraries. Ask for the person in charge of programming. You probably won't sell many books at a library, if any, but it's a chance to get publicity and generate interest. And you can always tell your audience where your books are available. Bring business cards! Have a drawing for a signed copy of your book.

BOOK LAUNCH PARTY: Depending on the funds you have at your disposal, you can hold a book launch. Cookies, sodas, punch. Put together a door prize–a free copy of the book at a minimum or a basket full of surprises that relate to your book—Harry Potter brand candies, a toy wand, tickets to a local movie theatre for a superhero movie and don't forget to tuck a copy of your book in there, too. If you can't locate a book store that can or will host, think of other venues. If your book is aimed at the 18-to-34 year old market, perhaps a local bar that has a back room. To keep the cost minimal, you could arrange a cash bar and just buy a few inexpensive hors d'oerves. Maybe a video arcade as a venue?

CELEBRITIES: Actors to Locate 1-800-503-6737. What about gamers? Extreme sports stars? A movie star who starred in a fantasy movie? You can ask for up to four actors. They will give you their agent's phone number and name. From there, ask if they have a manager or publicist. If not, work with the talent agent's assistant. Write down what you want to say and stick to it. Get a contact email address and follow up the phone call with an email note. If you want to pitch your book to a particular celebrity, ask the assistant how to do that.

CONTESTS: Be careful of entering contests. Do research to see they are actually offering more than just a chance to be edited or get an agent. Don't pay a lot for the average contest. The odds are not great and there isn't a lot of prestige attached to the majority of them. If they want you to pay for your plaque or trophy, they aren't really worth the cost. Publication in a regional magazine and several copies of the publication can be a terrific prize. Also check out writers groups and associations in your area.

WHERE TO LOOK: Do a google search for fantasy and scifi book clubs, gamer groups, etc… Be very selective on anything you pay to join and be careful when you search.

Tip #110. The Promo.

These are the fun little gimmicks authors give out to promote their books or their brands. Key chains, bookmarks, beach balls, geocaching coins—I've even seen an author promote a book set in the sixties with a vinyl record. Go for the unusual that will attract attention and cause someone walking by your table at a book fair to stop and turn around. Don't just order from the first site you see. Do some research. Prices vary widely. It's not necessary to pay a lot to get your message in the hands of possible readers in a fun way.

Tip #111. Have a birthday party for your book!

As touched on in the Sample Marketing Plan above, the book launch is a party. Plan this as soon as you have a publication date. This can be held at a restaurant, country club, book store, museum, library—anywhere you choose. Think about the setting of your book and be creative. Bookstores have the advantage of salespeople who can handle book sales while you speak and sign autographs, but you may be able to make arrangements with a local bookstore to send a bookseller to your event with their stock of your book.

Advertise your book launch anywhere possible. A book about a pet? Call veterinarian offices in the area and see if they would be willing to put up a flyer. A children's book? Send your flyer to local schools. A history book? Contact local history museums, clubs and organizations. A mystery? How about a house that has a reputation of being haunted?

What's in a book launch? Light refreshments are a nice touch. Wine and cheese, cookies, or hors d'oerves. Whether it's casual or a fancy affair is up to you, your venue and your budget. Is your book set on a cruise? How about tropical punch and palm tree shaped cookies? Now's a great time to roll out those promo products. Beach balls? Plastic sunglasses? Lip balm? Whatever you choose, make sure you get either your name or the name of your book, and your website address, on everything!

Tip #112. Self-publishing vs. traditional publishing marketing.

There are obviously differences in the marketing support the author can expect in each of these two routes to publishing.

A traditional publisher may send out news releases and possibly work to book speaking engagements for you. They may prepare posters and postcards. The support isn't a given, though. Be sure to read your contract carefully to see what your publisher is offering and make sure you understand the cost. Publishers are obviously in the business to make money. It's possible your contract will include a certain number of promotional materials and anything over that amount will be on your dime. Other publishers will bill you from the very beginning.

In the wonderful world of self-publishing, you're pretty much on your own. Sites like Createspace provide you a free author's page and will list your book for sale on Amazon.com, but that's where the free support ends. For an additional fee, sites like Createspace will have a professional copywriter work on your back cover material and the author biography.

NOTES:

_____

_____

_____

_____

_____

_____

_____

_____

_____

_____

_____

_____

_____

_____

_____

CHAPTER 14: AFTER YOUR BOOK IS PUBLISHED

Congratulations! You are holding a copy of your own published book in your hands. There's your name—right on the cover. It's an overwhelming feeling, right? You've made it farther than most people who dream of writing a book. And what do you do now? Marketing kicks into high gear. Your goal is to get your book in front of as many people as you can without driving your friends away.

Tip #113. Another Business Card?

You'll probably want more than one. Why? One will be your author card—the one that announces that you're a writer or an author. Keep it simple. A card loaded with quotes or artwork is not as easy to read as one with just a logo and your name and contact information.

The second, third and fourth may be separate business cards for each of your books. Using a copy of your book cover is eye-catching. Add your contact information, or blurbs about the book, to the back.

One of the neatest ways to link someone holding your card to your website (where they can purchase your book) is a QR code. These are squares filled with black lines. When scanned by a cell phone, it will open your website. Easy! Where do you get one? Companies that print business cards are now offering these as a free or low-cost option.

Tip #114. Talk, Talk, Talk.

Many authors don't enjoy standing in front of a group of people and talking about themselves and their books can be intimidating. It is, however, something you'll have to get used to. Readers love buying books from someone they've heard speak. The chance to have an author sign a book can be thrilling—especially if it's an author a reader has been following for a while.

And how do you get these speaking engagements? If your work has been published by a traditional publisher, you'll get a little help here. The marketing department of your publisher will send out news releases on your behalf and direct interest to you. If you're real lucky, they'll go beyond that and actually book speaking engagements.

Ok, but I'm self-published. What now? Here's a few suggestions. Contact:

1. The events coordinator at your local library
2. Condominium and homeowner associations
3. Churches, synagogues, retirement communities
4. Local women's groups, business groups, Chambers of Commerce
5. If your book concerns history, contact local historical societies
6. Children's book? Contact local schools, after care programs
7. Book about a pet? Contact local shelters and pet rescues
8. Local television stations might be interested
9. Local radio stations
10. Newspapers

In the world of the internet, these lists are readily available at the touch of a button. Don't be concerned that they might tell you no. It's highly likely that most of them will. Be prepared and don't stress over it. Just contact another group and keep working on it.

Tip #115. Ok, I've got the talk booked. Now what?

The last thing you want to do is stand at a podium and recite a prepared speech. You want to engage your audience as much as possible. If you've written a non-fiction book, prepare a power point presentation or have video clips to help tell your tale. If not possible, add humor to your talk where appropriate.

Practice, practice, practice until you almost have your talk memorized. You don't want to memorize it, though. That leads into reciting instead of sharing. I found my three cats to be a very helpful practice audience. I've also stood in front of the mirror practicing gestures and facial expressions until I was extremely comfortable with what I felt needed to be said.

Choose your book excerpt carefully based on the group. An adult passage is more appropriate for an evening book club than a high school auditorium.

Generally, a good formula for your talk is as follows:
1. Who you are and how you came to write this particular book;
2. An excerpt from the book;
3. Questions and answers.

I wrote a non-fiction book about my disabled cat. In between No. 1 and 2, I have my audience stand, hold up one foot and balance to help them learn about the disability. I show a few video clips of the cat walking and a clip art of a cat's brain. By the time I'm reading from the book, they understand the situation and enjoy the story more.

For the history book I wrote, I share pictures from the book and talk about that specific point in time. The pictures help me keep on topic.

Always ask the coordinator how much time you are allotted and tailor your speech to fit their requirements. Make sure to allow time for questions and answers.

Start drafting the speech by putting in everything you'd like to say. Then cut out what's necessary to meet the time constraint.

Tip #116. How do I get a book review?

Your book is out and you wait anxiously for the first review of your stunning masterpiece from someone you aren't related to or who doesn't know you from elementary school. And you wait. And wait.

How do these other authors get someone to comment?

Here are a few ideas:

1.   Ask. Ask on your blog, ask at your book launch, ask at your book talks. If you ask enough people someone will eventually post a comment for you.

2.   Give a few books away with the request that the only requirement is that they post an honest review. You cannot ask for a good review, just an honest one.

3.   Services are available that will review your book and provide an honest review for a price. These can range from a few dollars up to hundreds. Be very careful with these. You could end up paying a lot of money for something that doesn't bring much of a return, i.e. new readers.

Tip #117. What do I do about a bad book review?

You poured your very soul into your book. Your agent loved it. The editor loved it. You've received wonderful reviews. And then, it happens. Someone posts a bad review. You read it with your jaw on your chest. How could someone not see the genius?

It happens. Part of what makes humans unique is that every single person reads a book from his or her individual perspective. Readers have their own life experiences and beliefs and sometimes that leads them to dislike what you've written.

Don't log on immediately to rebut their post. Back away from the computer. Call your writer friends and vent. Rant and rave for a few minutes. Then go on about promoting your book and writing the next one. You can't please everyone. Just let it go.

Tip #118. Would a writing conference help me market?

Absolutely.

Not only do a lot of them offer opportunities to learn the craft or how to sell your manuscript, a lot of them offer seminars on marketing. Accept the handouts, take notes and pay attention. Writers' conferences, associations and seminars are the best places to learn about trends. Is Facebook surging? What about Twitter—would that work for you? Is there a new site on the horizon that would be even better? If you aren't into searching the internet and keeping up on the twists and turns of the marketing and writing world by yourself, this is the best way to keep abreast of the ebbs and flows of this particular river.

Tip #119. Critique groups.

Of course for learning the craft, but for marketing? Are you nuts?

It's been rumored, but this isn't quite as crazy as it sounds. A critique group is usually made up of people who are somewhat serious about honing their writing skills. If you're fortunate, the group you join will have everyone from the "just picked up the pencil after 40 years" to the "just published his fourth novel." Those who have been where you are right now are usually happy to share their experiences—both good and bad—to help you find your way through the first time.

You've learned you're going to need a synopsis and a query letter to send to agents and/or editors. Who better to review these two items and provide you with their honest opinions? The author biography? Yes, they can help with that. That text for the back of the book? Sure!

You'll discover that most writers are only too happy to help someone else through the maze and will often go past a simple critique to connect you with an expert or two they may have found in their last trip.

Tip #120. Don't blink.

Never be afraid to ask. The most anyone can ever do is tell you no. If you ask the local television station if they might be interested in interviewing a local author about the book he just wrote, they might just say yes. Understand that every "no" puts you closer to a "yes" and don't let it discourage you.

NOTES:_____

_____

_____

_____

_____

_____

_____

_____

_____

_____

_____

_____

_____

_____

CHAPTER 15: WHAT THE WRITER'S BEST DRESSED BOOKSHELF IS WEARING
References and Sources

Tip #121. Books about plotting books.

Excellent books have been written about plotting and if plotting is your weak spot, check them out. *How to Write Plots That Sell* by F.A. Rockwell is terrific. It's published by Contemporary Books, Inc. Another personal favorite is *Steal This Plot* by June and William Noble, published by Paul S. Eriksson. Still another helpful tome is *Plot* published by Writer's Digest Books.

Tip #122. Handy reference books to have in your writing library.

Craft:

Revision by Kit Reed, Writer's Digest Books
A Writer's Guide to Research by Lois Horowitz, Writer's Digest Books
The Synonym Finder by J.I. Rodale, Warner Books
Becoming A Writer by Dorothea Brande (absolutely invaluable to help you understand the writing process)
How to Use Writer's Block by Victoria Lincoln, Writer's Digest Books
How to Write Plots That Sell by F.A. Rockwell, Contemporary Books, Inc.
Steal This Plot by June and William Noble, Paul S. Ericksson, Publisher
Make That Scene by William Noble, Paul S. Eriksson, Publisher
Plot by Ansen Dibell, Writer's Digest Books
Get That Novel Started (And Keep It Going 'Til You Finish) by Donna Levin, Writer's Digest Books
On Writing by Stephen King, Pocket Books
Hooked: Write Fiction That Grabs Readers at Page One and Never Lets Them Go by Les Edgerton, Writer's Digest Books
The Art of Subtext by Charles Baxter, Graywolf Press

Hit Lit, Cracking the Code of The Twentieth Century's Biggest Bestsellers by James W. Hall, Random House Trade Paperbacks

Reference:

Bartlett's Quotations
Roget's Thesaurus
Dictionary of Fictional Characters by Martin Seymour-Smith, The Writer, Inc. (Great source for names and ideas)
   Books of poetry
   Encyclopedias
   A good reference for costumes and/or fashion design; *Costume in Context* by Jennifer Ruby, B.T. Batsford, London (This is a series you might find in the children's section of your library, but it's good.)
   The Historical Encyclopedia of Costumes by Albert Racinet, Facts on File Publications
   The Historical Encyclopedia of Fashion by Ludmilla Kybalova, et al, Hamlyn Publishers
   A reference book on architecture; I like *Houses: The illustrated Guide to Construction, Design and Systems* by Henry S. Harrison, published by the National Association of Realtors
   The Positive Trait Thesaurus: A Writer's Guide to Character Attributes by Angela Ackerman and Becca Puglisi, JADD Publishing, 2013.
   The Negative Trait Thesaurus: A Writer's Guide to Character Flaws by Angela Ackerman and Becca Puglisi, JADD Publishing, 2013.
   The Emotion Thesaurus: A Writer's Guide to Character Expression by Angela Ackerman and Becca Puglisi, writershelpingwriters.net 2012.

Marketing:

1001 Ways to Market Your Books by John Kremer
   Rise of the Machines—Human Authors in a Digital World by Kristen Lamb, ANA International; 1st edition (June 27, 2013)
   Jeff Herman's Guide to Book Publishers, Editors and Literary Agents: Who They Are, What They Want, How to Win Them Over by Jeff Herman, New World Library 2016

Tip #123. Magazines you should read and/or subscribe to, if you can afford them. If not, check out your local library.

Publisher's Weekly—Gives you current information on the publishing industry.
   Romantic Times—Great for romance and horror writers both from a standpoint of marketing and market information and promotion for your books.
   Mystery Scene—Lots of good information on mystery, science fiction, horror and fantasy markets and current books.
   Science Fiction Chronicle—The bible for science fiction, horror and fantasy.
   The Writer—Contains good information about writing techniques.
   Writer's Digest—Offers good information on writing and marketing.
   Poets & Writers—Especially valuable if you are writing literary materials.

Guerilla Marketing for Writers by Jay Conrad Levinson, Rich Frishman, Michael Larson—An absolute must.
Small Press Review
Futures Mysterious Anthology Magazine

Tip #124. Writers' organizations worth exploring.

Successful writers spend the majority of their time writing and marketing; however, they also network and that networking does double duty. Additionally, it provides an essential social outlet which is vital because writing is truly a lonely business—and usually only another writer understands the insecurities and anxieties of the writing life.

Networking is also good for business because many writers will share information about agents, editors, publishers and new markets. They network quite often by joining organizations composed of writers working in the same genres. Knowing other, more successful writers can also be helpful to the novice in that the more established writer may be willing to write a cover blurb for you. The following is a partial list of organizations for the serious writer. Visit their websites to obtain membership information:

Horror Writers of America
Mystery Writers of America
National Association of Women Writers
Poetry Society of America
Private Eye Writers of America
Romance Writers of America
Science Fiction Writers of America
Sisters in Crime
Small Press, Writers and Artists Organization
WANA International
Western Writers of America
Women Writing the West
Women's National Book Association

Tip #125. Interesting websites to check out:

http://writing.shawguides.com/
https://canadianauthors.org/national/
http://www.infinitypublishing.com/author-resources/
http://screenwriter.com/insider/WritersCalendar.html
http://hwg.org/opcenter/events/
http://www.writersdigest.com/contests
http://www.cinestory.org/
http://humorwriters.org/Contest.html
http://poetshouse.org/aboutlinks.htm
http://www3.sympatico.ca/susanio/WWClinks.html
http://writers-editors.com/

http://writersweekly.com/
https://www.pw.org/

Tip #126 Writer's Conferences.

The following are just a few conferences and sources for writers' conferences. There are several local, regional, national and international conferences held that focus on different genres as well as general workshops on the craft and business of writing:

- *Killer Nashville International Writers' Conference*
- *Sleuthfest*, Mystery Writers' of America
- *writing.shawguides.com* lists several throughout the United States and even a few international conferences.
- Eckerd College's *Writers in Paradise*
- *Poets and Writers* Magazine is also a good source for up-to-date conference and workshop listings.
- *Writer's Digest Annual Conference*
- *Annual Florida Writers Conference*, Florida Writers Association

NOTES:_____

_____

_____

_____

_____

_____

_____

_____

_____

_____

_____

_____

_____

_____

WORKSHEETS

CHARACTER NOTES

Character Names	Roles
Example: Sue Smith	Heroine

BLANK CALENDAR

Month:					Year:	
Sunday	Monday	Tuesday	Wednesday	Thursday	Friday	Saturday

AN OUTLINE TO HELP PLOT YOUR NOVEL

Your working title: _____

Prologue:

Date: _____ Time: _____ Place: _____

Point of view character, if applicable: _____

Action that takes place: _____

_____

_____

_____

Chapter 1, Scene 1:

Date: _____ Time: _____ Place: _____

Point of view character, if applicable: _____

What happens: _____

_____

_____

_____

Chapter _____, Scene _____:

Date: _____ Time: _____ Place: _____

How much time elapsed since scene 1: _____

Point of view character, if applicable: _____

What happens: _____

_____

_____

_____

Chapter _____, Scene _____:

Date: _____ Time: _____ Place: _____

How much time elapsed since previous scene: _____

Point of view character, if applicable: _____

What happens: _____

_____

_____

_____

Chapter _____, Scene _____:

Date: _____ Time: _____ Place: _____

How much time elapsed since previous scene: _____

Point of view character, if applicable: _____

What happens: _____

_____

_____

_____

Chapter _____, Scene _____:

Date: _____ Time: _____ Place: _____

How much time elapsed since previous scene: _____ _____

Point of view character, if applicable: _____

What happens: _____

_____

_____

_____

Employment Application for Hero

If you take the time to really think about your characters and answer these questions, you'll create believable characters.

Name and nicknames: _____

Height: _____ Weight: _____ Color and shape of eyes: _____

_____

Hair color and texture: _____

Shape of face: _____

Shape of chin: _____ Nose: _____

Mouth: _____ Forehead: _____ Cheekbones: _____

How does he physically/facially express/repress his anger? _____

_____

How does he express embarrassment? _____

_____

How does he express joy? _____

_____

How does he express fear? _____

_____

How does he express affection and love? _____

_____

How does he express impatience? _____

_____

_____

Scars: _____ Build and attitude toward body: _____

_____

_____

Date of birth: _____ Time: _____AM/PM Sign: _____

Place of birth: _____

Name of hospital: _____

Address: _____

Delivering doctor: _____ Nurse: _____

Mother's maiden name: _____

Father's name: _____

Sisters or brothers? If so, ages and names: _____

_____

First home address: _____

Father's occupation: _____

Mother's occupation: _____

Childhood traumas? Injuries and scars, impairments, deaths in the family, serious changes in family's status: _____

_____

Family pets, names, types and ages when hero had them: _____

_____

_____

Hero's relationship with mother: _____

_____

_____

_____

Hero's relationship with father: _____

_____

_____

_____

Hero's relationship with sister: _____

_____

_____

Hero's relationship with brother: _____

_____

_____

What was the general atmosphere in the hero's childhood home? Happy? Loving? Tense? Hostile? Fearful? Supportive? _____

_____

_____

Any significant event (good or bad) in the hero's first six years? _____

_____

_____

Any childhood illnesses? If so, what were they, how were they treated, how did he react to being ill and were there any lasting effects? _____

_____

_____

How old is hero when he starts school? _____

What is the name of this school and what is its address? _____

_____

What does it look like? What section of town is it in? _____

_____

_____

What is the hero's attitude toward starting school? Excited? Scared? _____

_____

What is the name of his first teacher? _____

What is the name of his favorite teacher and why is this teacher so special in his life? _____

_____

_____

What is the name of his least favorite teacher/principal and why is their relationship negative?

_____

_____

_____

Who were his best friends in school? Names and descriptions: _____

_____

Adventures, mishaps they experienced: _____

_____

_____

_____

_____

What hobbies did (and does) the hero have? _____

_____

What were his best subjects? _____

_____

What were his worst subjects? _____

_____

What was the name of the middle/junior high school he attended? Where was it located? _____

_____

How did hero approach puberty? How did he get through having his voice change, for example. What was his most embarrassing experience during this period: _____

_____

_____

_____

_____

Did he have a girlfriend in middle school? What was his attitude toward girls? _____

_____

_____

_____

How did he spend his time after school? _____

_____

_____

What chores did he have to do? _____

_____

_____

_____

How did he spend his weekends? Did his family go to church on Sunday? _____

_____

What did he want to grow up to be? _____

_____

What was his favorite song and musician? _____

_____

What was his favorite movie? _____

Who was his favorite movie star? _____

What was his favorite TV show? _____

_____

Who was his favorite TV star? _____

What was his favorite book? _____

_____

What was and is his favorite meal? _____

_____

_____

How did he feel about sports? _____

_____

_____

What was his favorite sport? _____

_____

Who was his favorite athlete? _____

What high school did hero attend? Name and address: _____

_____

What did school look like? How big and architectural style: _____

_____

_____

_____

Did hero graduate? If so, standing in class? _____

_____

_____

Was he active in sports? If so, which one, what position did he play and how good was he?

_____

_____

What was the outstanding game/bout/competition in his high school career? _____

_____

_____

_____

Did he enjoy high school or was he impatient to get out and get on with living? Was he popular? Did he hold a class office? Was he a member of the National Honor Society? _____

_____

_____

_____

Did he date? Did he have a girlfriend? Who was she? Was she popular? What kind of personality/character did she have? What did she look like? Why did they break up? How long did they go together? What kind of relationship did they have? How did he get along with girls? Was he shy? Self-confident? Self-controlled? _____

_____

_____

_____

_____

Who were his enemies and why? _____

_____

_____

_____

Did he ever get in trouble with his family and/or the law? If so, what were the circumstances and consequences? _____

_____

_____

_____

_____

What clubs was he a member of? How did he spend his time after school? Did he have a job? If so, what was it? _____

_____

_____

_____

_____

Did hero go to college? If so, which one and where was it? _____

_____

What did he major in? What kind of work did he want to do when he graduated? _____

_____

Did he graduate? If so, when and what was his standing in class? _____

_____

Was he a member of a fraternity? If so, which one? _____

_____

Did he have a car? If so, what kind? What color? What year? What was his attitude toward it?

_____

_____

Any funny or interesting experiences with the car? Have a nickname? Model? Appearance?

_____

_____

Now that he's out in the world, what work does he do? _____

_____

What is the name of the company / business he works for? _____ _____

_____

What is the address of the company? _____

_____

What is the name of his employer or, if he is the boss, who is his right-hand person? _____

_____

_____

How does he now spend his free time and weekends? _____

_____

_____

Is he married? Divorced? Engaged? Dating? _____

_____

What is his attitude toward his marriage/divorce? _____

_____

_____

Where does he live now? House? Apartment? Hotel? Address: _____

_____

What does it look like? Is his home important to him? Is it well kept? Neglected? And what is there about the home that expresses his character and outlook on life? _____

_____

_____

_____

_____

_____

What clubs/lodges/organizations/charities is he a member of now or involved with? _____

_____

_____

What kind of clothing does he like to wear? _____

_____

_____

What's his favorite color? _____

_____

What's his favorite drink? Snack food? _____

_____

_____

_____

What political party does he belong to? Is he politically active? Is he a patriot? How does he feel about politicians? Is he active locally? Nationally? Statewide? _____

_____

_____

_____

How does he feel about religion? Is he a member of a church? How does he feel about God? Is he active in church? _____

_____

_____

_____

What is his attitude toward money? Does he covet it? Is he greedy? Does he spend freely? Does he save regularly? Does he respect it or consider it evil? What kind of a tipper is he? _____

_____

_____

_____

_____

_____

_____

What are the things that anger him? _____

_____

What would he lie about? _____

_____

_____

_____

What is his relationship like with his parents and siblings now? Does he visit his parents regularly?

_____

_____

_____

_____

_____

What is his parents' attitude toward him? _____

_____

What is his wife's/girlfriend's attitude toward him? _____

_____

_____

What are his weaknesses and flaws? _____

_____

_____

_____

What are his strengths? _____

_____

_____

_____

Is he neat and tidy or sloppy in his dress and thinking? Is he organized or scattered? Is he focused or determined? _____

_____

_____

_____

If your hero has absolutely nothing to do, absolutely free time, how will he spend it? _____

_____

_____

_____

What was the happiest time in his life? _____

_____

_____

_____

_____

_____

What was the saddest? _____

_____

_____

_____

_____

_____

What was his greatest triumph? _____

_____

_____

_____

What was his greatest defeat? _____

_____

_____

_____

_____

_____

_____

How did he react to that defeat? _____

_____

_____

_____

_____

_____

Notes of things to research: _____

_____

_____

_____

_____

_____

Employment Application for Heroine

If you take the time to really think about your characters and answer these questions, you'll create believable characters.

Name and nicknames: _____

Height: _____ Weight: _____ Color and shape of eyes: _____

_____

Hair color and texture: _____

Shape of face: _____

Shape of chin: _____ Nose: _____

Mouth: _____ Forehead: _____ Cheekbones: _____

Typical expression on face: _____

How does she physical/facially express/repress her anger? _____

_____

How does she express embarrassment? _____

_____

How does she express joy? _____

_____

How does she express fear? _____

_____

_____

How does she express affection and love? _____

_____

How does she express impatience? _____

_____

_____

Scars: _____ Build and attitude toward body: _____

_____

_____

Date of birth: _____ Time: ____-_____AM/PM Sign: _____

Place of birth: _____

Name of hospital: _____

Address: _____

Delivering doctor: _____ Nurse: _____

Mother's maiden name: _____ _____ __

Father's name: _____

Sisters or brothers? If so, ages and names: _____

_____

First home address: _____

Father's occupation: _____

Mother's occupation: _____

Childhood traumas? Injuries and scars, deaths in the family, serious changes in family's status:

_____

_____

_____

Family pets, names, types and ages when heroine had them: _____

_____

Heroine's relationship with mother: _____

_____

_____

_____

Heroine's relationship with father: _____

_____

_____

_____

Heroine's relationship with sister: _____

_____

_____

_____

Heroine's relationship with brother: _____

_____

_____

_____

What was the general atmosphere in the heroine's childhood home? Happy? Loving? Tense? Hostile? Fearful? Supportive? _____

_____

_____

Any significant event (good or bad) in the heroine's first six years? _____

_____

_____

_____

Any childhood illnesses? If so, what were they, how were they treated, how did she react to being ill and were there any lasting effects? _____

_____

_____

_____

How old is heroine when she starts school? _____

What is the name of this school and what is its address? _____

_____

What does it look like? What section of town is it in? _____

_____

_____

What is the heroine's attitude toward starting school? Excited? Scared? _____

_____

What is the name of her first teacher? _____

What is the name of her favorite teacher and why is this teacher so special in her life? _____

_____

_____

What is the name of her least favorite teacher / principal and why is their relationship negative?

_____

_____

Who were her best friends in school? Names and descriptions: _____

_____

_____

_____

Adventures, mishaps they experienced: _____

_____

_____

_____

_____

_____

_____

What hobbies did (and does) the heroine have? _____

_____

What were her best subjects? _____

_____

What were her worst subjects? _____

_____

What was the name of the middle/junior high school she attended? Where was it located? _____

_____

How did the heroine approach puberty? How did she get through having her first period, development of a bosom, for example. What was her most embarrassing experience during this period: _____

_____

_____

_____

Did she have a boyfriend in middle school? What was her attitude toward boys? _____

_____

_____

How did she spend her time after school? _____

_____

What chores did she have to do? _____

_____

_____

_____

How did she spend her weekends? Did her family go to church on Sunday? _____

_____

_____

What did she want to grow up to be? _____

_____

What was her favorite song and musician? _____

_____

What was her favorite movie? _____

Who was her favorite movie star? _____

What was her favorite TV show? _____

_____

Who was her favorite TV star? _____

What was her favorite book? _____

_____

What was and is her favorite meal? _____

_____

_____

_____

How did she feel about sports? _____

_____

_____

What was her favorite sport? _____

_____

Who was her favorite athlete? _____

What high school did heroine attend? Name and address: _____

_____

_____

What did school look like? Size and architectural style: _____

_____

_____

_____

Did heroine graduate? If so, standing in class? _____

_____

_____

Was she active in sports? If so, which one, what position did she play and how good was she?

_____

_____

_____

_____

What was the outstanding game/bout/competition in her high school career? _____

_____

_____

_____

Did she enjoy high school or was she impatient to get out and get on with living? Was she popular? Did she hold a class office? Was she a member of the National Honor Society?

_____

_____

_____

_____

Did she have a date for the senior prom? Did she have a good time? Did she have any interesting experiences? What did she wear? _____

_____

_____

_____

_____

What perfume did she wear? _____

Did she date? Did she have a boyfriend? Who was he? Was he popular? What kind of personality/character did he have? What did he look like? Why did they break up? How long did they go together? What kind of relationship did they have? How did she get along with boys? Was she shy? Self-confident? Self-controlled? _____

_____

_____

_____

_____

Who were her enemies and why? _____

_____

_____

_____

Did she ever get in trouble with her family and/or the law? What were the circumstances and consequences? Was she mischievous? A tomboy? Quiet? Devious? What would she lie about?

_____

_____

_____

_____

What clubs was she a member of? How did she spend her time after school? Did she have a job? If so, what was it? _____

_____

_____

_____

Did heroine go to college? If so, which one and where was it? _____

_____

What did she major in? What kind of work did she want to do when she graduated? _____

_____

Did she graduate? If so, when and what was her standing in class? _____

_____

Was she a member of a sorority? If so, which one? _____

_____

Did she have a car? If so, what kind? What color? What year? What was her attitude toward it?

_____

_____

Any funny or interesting experiences with the car? Did it have a nickname? Distinguishing features?

_____

_____

_____

Now that she's out in the world, what work does she do? _____

_____

What is the name of the company/business she works for? _____

_____

What is the address of the company? _____

_____

What is the name of her employer or, if she is the boss, who is her right-hand person? _____

_____

How does she now spend her free time and weekends? _____

_____

_____

Is she married? Divorced? Engaged? Dating? If so, who? _____

_____

What is her attitude toward her marriage / divorce / relationships? _____

_____

_____

Does she have children? What is her attitude toward having children? _____

_____

_____

Where does she live now? House? Apartment? Hotel? Address: _____

_____

_____

_____

What does it look like? Is her home important to her? Is it well kept? Neglected? And what is there about the home that expresses her character and outlook on life? _____

_____

_____

_____

_____

_____

What clubs/lodges/organizations/charities is she a member of now or involved with? _____

_____

_____

What kind of clothing does she like to wear? _____

_____

_____

What's her favorite color? _____

_____

What's her favorite perfume? _____

What's her favorite drink? Snack food? _____

What political party does she belong to? Is she politically active? Is she a patriot? How does she feel about politicians? Is she active locally? Nationally? Statewide? _____

_____

_____

_____

_____

How does she feel about religion? Is she a member of a church? How does she feel about God? Is she active in church? Did she sing in the choir? Teach Sunday School? _____

_____

_____

_____

What is her attitude toward money? Does she covet it? Is she greedy? Does she spend freely? Does she save regularly? Does she respect it or consider it evil? What kind of a tipper is she?

_____

_____

_____

_____

_____

What are the things that anger her? _____

_____

What is her relationship like with her parents and siblings now? Does she visit his parents regularly?

_____

_____

_____

_____

_____

What is her parents' attitude toward her? _____

_____

_____

_____

What is her husband's/boyfriend's attitude toward her? _____

_____

_____

_____

What are her weaknesses and flaws? _____

_____

_____

_____

What are her strengths? _____

_____

Is she neat and tidy or sloppy in her dress and thinking? Is she organized or scattered? Is she focused or determined? _____

_____

_____

_____

If your heroine has absolutely nothing to do, absolutely free time, how will she spend it?

_____

_____

_____

_____

What was the happiest time in her life? _____

_____

_____

_____

_____

What was the saddest? _____

_____

_____

_____

_____

_____

What was her greatest triumph? _____

_____

_____

_____

_____

_____

What was her greatest defeat? _____

_____

_____

_____

_____

How did she react to that defeat? _____

_____

_____

_____

_____

How does she feel about being a woman? _____

_____

_____

_____

Notes of things to research: _____

_____

_____

_____

_____

_____

_____

_____

_____

_____

HELPFUL ET CETERAS

How did the hero and heroine meet? _____

_____

_____

First reaction to one another? _____

_____

_____

How to hero and/or heroine first meet villain? _____

_____

_____

Where do they meet? _____

_____

_____

What is the hero and/or heroine's first reaction to villain? _____

_____

_____

What is the villain's reaction to each of them in the middle and end of the book? _____

_____

_____

Employment Application for Villain

**If you take the time to really think about your villain and
answer these questions, you'll create believable characters.**

Name and nicknames: _____

Height: _____ Weight: _____ Color and shape of eyes: _____

_____

Hair color and texture: _____

Shape of face: _____

Shape of chin: _____ Nose: _____

Mouth: _____ Forehead: _____ Cheekbones: _____

How does s/he physical/facially express/repress his anger? _____

_____

How does s/he express embarrassment? _____

_____

How does s/he express joy? _____

_____

How does s/he express fear? _____

_____

How does s/he express affection and love? _____

_____

How does s/he express impatience? _____

_____

_____

_____

_____

Scars: _____ Build and attitude toward body: _____

_____

_____

Date of birth: _____ Time: _____AM/PM Sign: _____

Place of birth: _____

Name of hospital: _____

Address: _____

Delivering doctor: _____ Nurse: _____

Mother's maiden name: _____

Father's name: _____

Sisters or brothers? If so, ages and names: _____

_____

First home address: _____

Father's occupation: _____

Mother's occupation: _____

Childhood traumas? Injuries and scars, deaths in the family, serious changes in family's status:

_____

_____

_____

Family pets, names, types and ages when villain had them: _____

_____

Villain's relationship with mother: _____

_____

_____

Villain's relationship with father: _____

_____

_____

_____

Villain's relationship with sister: _____

_____

_____

_____

Villain's relationship with brother: _____

_____

_____

What was the general atmosphere in the villain's childhood home? Happy? Loving? Tense? Hostile? Fearful? Supportive? _____

_____

Any significant event (good or bad) in the villain's first six years? _____

_____

_____

_____

Any childhood illnesses? If so, what were they, how were they treated, how did he react to being ill and were there any lasting effects? _____

_____

_____

_____

How old is villain when he starts school? _____

What is the name of this school and what is its address? _____

_____

What does it look like? What section of town is it in? _____

_____

_____

Was the villain's first day of school a positive or negative experience? What happened? How did that affect him/her? _____

_____

What is the name of his/her first teacher? _____

_____

How did s/he and this teacher feel about each other? _____

_____

What is the name of his/her least favorite teacher/principal and why is their relationship negative?

_____

_____

_____

Who were his/her best friends in school? Names and descriptions: _____

_____

Why were they friends? _____

_____

Adventures, mishaps they experienced: _____

_____

_____

_____

_____

What hobbies did (and does) the villain have? _____

_____

What were his/her best subjects? _____

_____

What were the worst subjects? _____

_____

How did villain approach puberty? How did he get through having his voice change, for example. What was his/her most embarrassing experience during this period: _____

_____

_____

_____

_____

What is his/her attitude toward the opposite sex? _____

_____

_____

What did s/he want to grow up to be? _____

_____

Who or what does s/he love? _____

_____

What is his/her attitude toward what s/he has accomplished in comparison to those childhood dreams? _____

_____

_____

_____

_____

What was his/her favorite movie? How did it impact your villain? _____

_____

Is your villain in total touch with reality? What mental quirks does your villain have? _____

_____

_____

_____

_____

_____

What was his/her favorite book? Why? _____

_____

_____

Did villain graduate from high school and college? If so, standing in class? What is his/her attitude toward education? Names of schools? _____

_____

_____

Was s/he active in sports? If so, which one, what position did s/he play and how good was s/he? Was s/he an honest or dishonest competitor? Did s/he fight fair? _____

_____

_____

_____

_____

What was the outstanding game/bout/competition in his/her high school career? _____

_____

Who were his/her enemies and why? _____

_____

_____

_____

_____

Did s/he ever get in trouble with his/her family and/or the law? If so, what were the circumstances and consequences?_____

_____

_____

_____

_____

_____

Was s/he a member of a sorority or fraternity? If so, which one? _____

_____

Now that s/he's out in the world, what work does s/he do? _____

_____

What is the name of the company/business s/he works for? _____

_____

What is the address of the company? _____

_____

What is the name of his/her employer or, if s/he is the boss, who is his/her right-hand person?

_____

_____

_____

How does s/he now spend his/her free time and weekends? _____

_____

_____

Is s/he married? Divorced? Engaged? Dating? _____

_____

What is his/her attitude toward his marriage/divorce? And if divorced, toward the ex? _____

_____

_____

_____

Where does s/he live now? House? Apartment? Hotel? Address: _____

_____

What does it look like? Is his/her home important to him/her? Is it well kept? Neglected? And what is there about the home that expresses his/her character and outlook on life? _____

_____

_____

_____

_____

_____

_____

What kind of a car does s/he drive now? Why this particular year and model? _____

_____

What clubs/lodges/organizations/charities is s/he a member of now or involved with? _____

_____

_____

_____

What kind of clothing does s/he like to wear and why? _____

_____

_____

_____

_____

What's his/her favorite color? _____

_____

What's his/her favorite drink? Snack food? _____

_____

_____

What political party does s/he belong to? Is s/he politically active? Is s/he a patriot? How does s/he feel about politicians? Is s/he active locally? Nationally? Statewide? _____

_____

_____

_____

_____

How does s/he feel about religion? Is s/he a member of a church? How does s/he feel about God? Is s/he active in church? _____

_____

_____

_____

What are his/her private demons? _____

_____

_____

_____

_____

What is his/her attitude toward money? Does s/he covet it? Is s/he greedy? Does s/he spend freely? Does s/he save regularly? Does s/he respect it or consider it evil? What kind of a tipper is s/he? _____

_____

_____

_____

_____

What angers him/her? _____

_____

What was his/her parents' attitude toward him/her and how did those color the person s/he's become? _____

_____

_____

_____

What are his/her weaknesses and flaws? _____

_____

_____

_____

What are his/her strengths? _____

_____

_____

_____

If your villain has absolutely nothing to do, absolutely free time, how will s/he spend it? _____

_____

_____

_____

What was the happiest time in his/her life? _____

_____

_____

_____

_____

_____

What was the saddest? _____

_____

_____

_____

_____

_____

_____

What was his/her greatest triumph? _____

_____

_____

_____

_____

_____

What was his/her greatest defeat? _____

_____

_____

_____

_____

_____

How did s/he react to that defeat? Is that what turned him/her into your villain?

_____

_____

_____

_____

_____

What does your villain want more than anything in the world? What keeps him/her awake nights? What will s/he do to accomplish his/her goals? How does s/he feel about other people's rights and dreams? _____

_____

_____

_____

When you are dealing with your villain, you need to know all of the above plus: What were the major disappointments in your villain's life that influenced his character? _____

_____

_____

_____

_____

What were three major items, positions, honors, people—your villain really wanted and failed to obtain or achieve? Or did achieve? _____

_____

_____

_____

_____

_____

_____

_____

_____

What were three or more situations in which your villain was severely disillusioned? _____

_____

_____

_____

_____

_____

_____

_____

What was the turning point in your villain's life, the point at which s/he became a villain as opposed to a hero/heroine? And how old was s/he? _____

_____

_____

_____

How does your villain display his or her disappointment? Anger? Grief? _____

_____

_____

_____

_____

_____

Summarize your villain's philosophy of life in one to three sentences? _____

_____

_____

_____

_____

Notes of things to research: _____

_____

_____

_____

_____

_____

_____

_____

_____

_____

_____

_____

_____

Checklist for Settings

Town/city/village name: _____

County or Parish or Province: _____

State and Country: _____

Population: _____ Does population vary seasonally? If so, how much? _____

_____

What type of government? _____

Who is the mayor? _____

Chairman of County Commissioners? _____

Who is Chief of Police? Sheriff? _____

Who is Fire Chief? _____

Who is State or District Attorney? _____

Coroner/Medical Examiner? _____

Where is the courthouse/city hall located? _____

What does it look like? Size, architectural style, age: _____

_____

What is the name of the hospital? _____

Where is it located? _____

What does it look like? Size architectural style, age: _____

_____

Is there a school in your book? What does it look like? What is the street address? What is the name? What is the name of the principal? _____

_____

_____

_____

_____

What is the name of the police/sheriff's department? Where is the headquarters located? What does it look like? What do the uniforms look like? How are the cars painted? Do they have a slogan or a motto? A town seal? What does it look like? _____

_____

_____

_____

_____

What are the town's main businesses? What kinds of businesses are they? What are their names? Where are they located? Are they seasonal or year-round? What impact do they have on the community? Do they hire mostly local people? _____

_____

_____

_____

_____

_____

_____

When was the town/village/city founded? And by whom? How does the town celebrate its founding? Does it have any special events—festivals honoring a famous citizen (the Thomas Edison Pageant of Light, for example) or a crop (the Azalea Festival or Garlic Festival). Does it have any special Christmas or Easter or Halloween customs? _____

_____

_____

_____

_____

_____

_____

What religion are the majority of the residents? What is the biggest church? And who is the minister/priest/rabbi? What is his/her name and what does s/he look like? What do the biggest churches look like? Where are these located—street address and section of town?

_____

_____

_____

_____

_____

_____

_____

What architectural styles are most common and in what different parts of town: Mediterranean, Victorian, Colonial? High rises, A-frames, ranch, bungalow? Other? _____

_____

_____

_____

_____

_____

What is the main form of public transportation? Bus? Subway? Cablecar? Taxi? What are the names? Where are the offices located? What do the vehicles look like? _____

_____

_____

_____

_____

_____

What is the name of the airport? Where is it located? What does it look like? How big is it?

_____

_____

_____

_____

What is the layout of the town like? Does it sprawl along the banks of a river or along a major highway? Is it designed around a town square? What are the names of the major streets and avenues? What are the major intersections? _____

_____

_____

_____

_____

Where is your community located within the state? And what are the nearest communities? How far is it from the state capitol? _____

_____

_____

_____

_____

_____

What is the major shopping center? What is its name? Where is it located? What is its architectural design? What color is it painted? How big is it? _____

_____

_____

_____

_____

_____

What statues or landmarks decorate the town? Where are they? Whom do they honor? Why were these people chosen? What are their names? Where are they located? _____

\
_____

\
_____

\
_____

\
_____

\
_____

What and where are the most popular restaurants—elegant, casual, picturesque and neighborhood? What are their names? Do they have a specialty of the house? Is there a food or foods for which the city is noted? _____

\
_____

\
_____

\
_____

\
_____

\
_____

\
_____

How do the residents of your town amuse themselves? Where are the amusement parks, the roller skating rinks, the movies, theaters, opera houses, sports centers? What are the names of these attractions? Are there specific tourist attractions? If so, what are they? _____

\
_____

\
_____

\
_____

\
_____

_____

_____

_____

What is your town's climate like? Is it subject to hurricanes, snowstorms, monsoons, tornadoes, earthquakes? Windy? How does this impact the citizens? The economy? _____

_____

_____

_____

_____

What is your town's rhythm? Bustling at 7:30 a.m. or quiet mornings and coming to life late in the afternoon? Is it hectic at noon when workers go into town for lunch and to shop? Or is it lively 24-hours a day? And what is responsible for this pace? _____

_____

_____

_____

_____

_____

_____

What is the overall atmosphere of the town? Sophisticated and metropolitan? Wealthy? Quiet, laid back? Working town? Resort town? Rural? _____

_____

_____

_____

_____

_____

_____

What is the general attitude of the citizens? Friendly? Helpful? Suspicious? Snobbish? Indifferent? Weary? _____

_____

_____

_____

What kind of people are these residents? Millionaires? Blue collar workers? Baby boomers? Educated? What minorities live in your town? Who are they? And how many are there? _____

_____

_____

_____

_____

What are the sounds of your community? Horns blaring and traffic? Birds singing? Train whistles? Planes taking off? Town clock? Church bells? _____

_____

_____

_____

What odors are unique or typical of your community? Gardenias? Tobacco—is there a cigarette manufacturer in town? Salt, if the community is right on the Gulf of Mexico? _____

_____

_____

_____

_____

What is your area like from the standpoint of topography? Beaches? Hills? Mountains? Valleys? Near a lake? A river? Lakes, rivers and mountains have names—what are they?

_____

_____

_____

_____

_____

What trees and shrubs grow in your town? Is the soil rich and fertile? Or sandy? What flowers grow and when do they bloom? _____

_____

_____

_____

_____

Notes to research: _____

_____

_____

_____

Interior Checklist

Relax! You won't have to go into such finite detail for every single room or chamber in which your characters interact, just the ones where they spend the most time. (Or the areas that are so unique the reader can't envision them.)

What are the approximate dimensions of the room? _____

What is the room's shape? _____

Where are the windows? _____

Where are the doors? _____

What are the major pieces of furniture and where are they positioned? _____

_____

_____

_____

_____

Any furniture with a personal story? _____

_____

_____

_____

_____

_____

_____

What style is the furniture? Victorian? Danish? Modern? Good Will retread?_____

_____

_____

_____

What condition is this furniture in? Well maintained? Shabby? Stained? _____

_____

_____

_____

If there are scars or marks on the furniture, how did they get there? _____

_____

_____

_____

What kind of floor does this room have? _____

What is the condition of the floor? _____

_____

Is it carpeted? If so, what does the carpet look like? Is it an Aubusson or a remnant or linoleum? And what condition is it in? What is the texture? What are the colors in it? _____

_____

_____

_____

_____

What colors are the walls? And are they painted? Wallpaper? If wallpaper, what pattern? Is there a molding in the room? _____

_____

_____

_____

_____

What about pictures? Are there any on the walls? Are they paintings or photographs or collages? Calendars? Are there plaques? If so, where are they and what do they look like? _____

_____

_____

_____

_____

_____

_____

_____

Any interesting stories about how your characters obtained these pictures? _____

_____

_____

_____

What about statuettes, clocks and smaller pieces of furniture? What do they look like and where are they positioned? Does your character have any special negative or cherished memories about any of these pieces? _____

_____

_____

_____

_____

_____

_____

What is the general atmosphere of the room? Cheery? Sterile? Brooding? Ominous? Inviting? Why?:

_____

_____

_____

_____

_____

_____

What about the housekeeping? Is it meticulous? Shoddy? Are the windows clean? _____

_____

_____

Notes to research: _____

_____

_____

_____

_____

_____

_____

_____

_____

_____

_____

_____

_____

_____

_____

_____

_____

_____

A WEEK IN THE LIFE OF

_____

(Your character's name)

Monday through Friday

7 a.m. to 8 a.m.: Your character arises. How? By alarm clock? Sun beating in his room? Is he cheerful or grouchy? Glad to be getting up? What does he do first? Make coffee? Brush his teeth? Grab a cigarette? Turn on the TV? What does he eat for breakfast or skip it? Does he watch TV? What does he watch? A news show? Does he grab the morning paper? Which paper? What does he read in it? Does he put out food for the dog or cat?_____

_____

_____

_____

_____

_____

_____

8 a.m. to 9 a.m.: He's on his way to work. How does he get there? Bus? Drive? What kind of car does he have? Subway? Where does he catch the bus or subway? What buildings and streets does he pass en route to his place of employment? How does he usually spend that time? Listening to his car radio? Thinking? Making notes for work? _____

_____

_____

_____

_____

_____

_____

9 a.m. to noon: What does he do first thing when he gets to work? Whom does he greet? Does he have any rituals? Does he take a coffee break? What does he actually, specifically do at his job?

_____

_____

_____

_____

_____

_____

_____

_____

Lunchtime: Where does he eat lunch? With whom? What does he order? If he goes out, what is the name of the restaurant? How does he get there? How long does he take? If he brown bags it, where does he eat on the premises? When and who made his lunch? Does he eat lunch with friends? Who are they? _____

_____

_____

_____

_____

_____

_____

_____

1 p.m. to 5 p.m.: What does he do in the afternoon? Does he take a break? Does he leave right on time? Work late? Leave early? Run errands on his way home? How does he get along with the people he works with? _____

_____

_____

_____

_____

_____

_____

_____

5 p.m. to 7 p.m.: What does he do when he first arrives home? Does he eat at home or stop off on his way home? Or drive through a Wendy's drive-through window? And when he gets home, does he change clothes? Take his shoes off? Read the mail? Mix a drink? What drink? _____

_____

_____

_____

_____

_____

_____

_____

_____

_____

7 p.m. to 12 p.m.: Dinner's over. Now what does he do? Does he load the dishwasher or do his own dishes? Or leave them for the cleaning woman? Does he have friends who drop by? Does he go to see friends? Does he do his laundry? Indulge in a hobby or a class? Go to a club or lodge meeting? Go to the movies? Does he have a special routine on Fridays? Does he date someone regularly on Fridays? Does he go to a specific cocktail lounge or restaurant? Or a concert?

_____

_____

_____

_____

_____

_____

_____

_____

Bedtime: What time does he usually go to bed? Does he have a regular routine? What is it? Does he sleep soundly? Is he restless? Does he toss and turn or sleep like the dearly deceased? Does he wear pajamas or sleep in the nude? _____

_____

_____

_____

_____

_____

_____

_____

_____

SATURDAY:

What does he do on Saturdays? Go SCUBA diving? Wash the car? Go grocery shopping? Do his laundry? Straighten the house or apartment? Go to a ball game? Visit his folks? Water the plants? Go to garage sales, flea markets or antique auctions? _____

_____

_____

_____

_____

_____

_____

SUNDAY:

Does he sleep late or get up at his usual time? Go to church? Plan a picnic? Go to the park? Go to the beach? _____

_____

_____

_____

_____

_____

_____

_____

_____

SUNDAY EVENING:

Does he get ready for work the next day? Stay out playing pool? Visit friends or have friends in? Go to an AA meeting? Pay his bills? Does he go to bed early? Late? What is his usual time to retire?

_____

_____

_____

_____

_____

_____

_____

_____

VACATION:

If your plot involves your character on a vacation, you may want to create a similar timeline so you'll know where he is and what he's doing. _____

_____

_____

_____

_____

_____

_____

Remember: You don't need to include all this information in your story, although you'll undoubtedly include some of it. The main purpose of this exercise is to help you get to know your characters.

NOTES:_____

_____

_____

_____

_____

_____

_____

_____

_____

_____

_____

_____

_____

_____

_____

_____

_____

_____

_____

_____

_____

_____

_____

_____

_____

_____

_____

_____

_____

_____

_____

_____

_____

ABOUT THE AUTHORS

PRUDY TAYLOR BOARD

Prudy Taylor Board is the author of 27 books and novels including *101 Tips on Writing and Selling Your First Novel.* The others include 3 horror novels, 2 murder mysteries and the remainder are regional histories ranging from the history of the Florida Sheriffs Youth Ranches to Barry University in Miami. Her career spans newspaper reporter to TV assignment editor/reporter, editor of two regional/lifestyle magazines. She also served as managing editor of the sales and marketing newsletters of Dartnell Corp. and personally edited *Selling and Sales and Marketing Executive Report* (then published by LRP Publications). Most recently, she was a project editor with Taylor & Francis Publishing, editing and producing STM books. She is now a freelance editor.

Prudy has taught various writing classes for more than 30 years. She has presented at writers' conferences not only throughout Florida, but coast-to-coast in the United States and internationally in Canada. Prudy's life has been writing since she was 9 years old. Walking home from elementary school one day and making up a story as she walked, she realized she was a writer, a scribe with stories to tell. Prudy is proud of her published books and has loved her career as an editor, reporter and TV news person. She attended and graduated from Stetson University and the University of Florida. She is equally proud of a shelf in a bookcase in her living room. That shelf contains memoirs and novels by other writers she has helped in both the writing and marketing of their books.

RUTH HARTMAN BERGE

Florida native Ruth Hartman Berge holds a degree in Business Administration from Florida State University where marketing was part of the curriculum. She was designing programs for high school choir productions from the age of 14.

She began writing short stories as a child and while still a paralegal by day in 2011, she became a professional writer when she began writing a monthly column called *The Florida You Don't Know* for Seabreeze Publications, Inc. After meeting Prudy Taylor Board later that year, she wrote and self-published a children's book about her disabled cat, *Betty Tales: The True Story of a Brave Bobblehead Cat.* Her next book, *Growing Up in Northern Palm Beach County: Boomer Memories from Dairy Belle to Double Roads,* was published by The History Press in 2016. Her short stories have been published in The Mensa Bulletin, the monthly magazine of American Mensa, and in the newsletter for the Treasure Coast Exotic Bird Club. She speaks to school age children about determination and persistence as often as possible and enjoys speaking about Palm Beach County history throughout South Florida.

Ruth designed her website and has assisted others in creating their websites, learning the joys of Search Engine Optimization (S.E.O.), and blogging as well as exploring how to market their books. She believes that book marketing in the age of the internet is constantly changing and the writer who never stops paying attention to internet trends will be the most successful in building a base of loyal fans and enjoying ever increasing book sales.